"I'll take homemade over store bought any day,
and that includes the family as well.
Cheryl gives us the tools and encouragement needed
to stay focused on that which is most important:
our family, our faith in Christ and the vision God has
placed in our hearts for a strong family.
This is a must-read for any person committed to staying home."

DR. RANDY CARLSON, president & host,
Parent Talk OnCall

"Down-to-earth, user-friendly, often humorous advice
to stay-at-home moms . . . plus
easy-to-follow instructions for joining the ranks.
Stay-at-Home Handbook is rich with motivation,
inspiration and practical how-to advice.
At a time when so many families are falling apart,
this affirming guide has become a welcome addition to my library
and deserves a home on the nightstand of every mother
who has found, or hopes to find, staying home to be as
valid a career choice as any other."

MARY HUNT, author of *Debt-Proof Living*
and *The Financially Confident Woman*

"Cheryl's expertise in maneuvering the obstacles of
stay-at-home motherhood fills each page of this book.
It is a must-read for any stay-at-home mom!"

JONNI MCCOY, author of *Miserly Moms*

"Cheryl Gochnauer understands the needs of the stay-at-home mom.
In this handbook you'll find the practical tips, strategies and
encouragement needed to make stay-at-home mothering all it can be!
It is a must for any woman committed to the profession of motherhood!"

JILL SAVAGE, author, *Professionalizing Motherhood,*
founder of Hearts at Home

"Being a stay-at-home mom at times can be
rewarding, frustrating, fulfilling, lonely and simply wonderful!
Cheryl understands its blessing and challenges firsthand,
so her strategies to help other mothers succeed in this
parenting path are practical, savvy and sound.
If you and your family are contemplating making this move,
you'll appreciate the balanced, insightful advice and handy resources
Stay-at-Home Handbook provides."

JANE JOHNSON STRUCK, editor, *Today's Christian Woman*

Stay-at-Home HANDBOOK

CHERYL GOCHNAUER

FOREWORD BY
DR. LAURA SCHLESSINGER

InterVarsity Press
Downers Grove, Illinois

Disclaimer

Opinions expressed by Cheryl Gochnauer and the individuals interviewed for this book are simply that—opinions. All advice should be weighed against your own abilities and circumstances and applied accordingly. It is up to the reader to determine if advice is safe and suitable for their personal situation. The author urges readers to meet with their own financial consultant and/or family counselor to work out the details of their individual and unique at-home experience.

InterVarsity Press
P.O. Box 1400, Downers Grove, IL 60515-1426
World Wide Web: www.ivpress.com
E-mail: mail@ivpress.com

©2002 by Cheryl Gochnauer

InterVarsity Press® is the book-publishing division of InterVarsity Christian Fellowship/ USA®, a student movement active on campus at hundreds of universities, colleges and schools of nursing in the United States of America, and a member movement of the International Fellowship of Evangelical Students. For information about local and regional activities, write Public Relations Dept., InterVarsity Christian Fellowship/USA, 6400 Schroeder Rd., P.O. Box 7895, Madison, WI 53707-7895, or visit the IVCF website at <www.ivcf.org>.

All Scripture quotations, unless otherwise indicated, are taken from the Holy Bible, New International Version®. NIV®. Copyright ©1973, 1978, 1984 by International Bible Society. Used by permission of Zondervan Publishing House. All rights reserved.

Chapter 36 originally appeared as a Today's Christian Woman article entitled "Super Stay-at-Home Mom" November/December 2001, pp. 74-77.

Cover photograph: Jon Feingersh/Corbis Stock Market

ISBN 0-8308-2336-0

Printed in the United States of America ∞

Library of Congress Cataloging-in-Publication Data
Gochnauer, Cheryl, 1958-
   Stay-at-home handbook: advice on parenting, finances, career, surviving each day, and much more/Cheryl Gochnauer; foreword by Laura Schlessinger.
     p. cm.
   ISBN 0-8308-2336-0 (paper: alk. paper)
   1. Mothers—Life skills guides. 2. Housewives—Life skills guides. 3. Parenting. 4. Home economics—Accounting. I. Title.
   HQ759 .G57 2002
   646.7'00852—dc21   *2001051943*

P	16	15	14	13	12	11	10	9	8	7	6	5	4	3	2	1
Y	13	12	11	10	09	08	07	06	05	04	03	02				

To truly enjoy life as an at-home parent,
you've got to have a great support system
that surrounds you with love
and empowers you for success.
I'd like to dedicate Stay-at-Home Handbook
to the inner loop of my own support system—
my wonderful husband, Terry,
and our precious girls, Karen and Carrie.
"I thank my God every time I remember you."
(PHILIPPIANS 1:3)

I hope Stay-at-Home Handbook *will be*
helpful to family-focused parents everywhere,
whether they are currently at home
or are working to get there someday.
God, bless our efforts as we
seize the opportunities available each day
to bond with the children you have given us.

Contents

PART 2 MANAGING YOUR MONEY

PART 3 EXAMINING YOUR WORK OPTIONS

PART 4 RAISING YOUR CHILDREN

PART 5 EXPLORING THEIR EDUCATION CHOICES

PART 6 GAINING YOUR SPOUSE'S SUPPORT

PART 7 HANDLING HOUSEHOLD RESPONSIBILITIES

PART 8 SHARING YOUR FAITH

Foreword

It's late June and there are unusually hot summer temperatures across the nation. Suddenly a wave of similar news stories begin to break—children, "accidentally" left in the family car by distracted parents and quickly succumbing to heat and dehydration, are dead. One busy mother, the CEO of a large hospital, "forgets" that her eight-month-old baby girl is strapped in her car seat in the back of the family van. As she is rushing to an important staff meeting, she fails to drop off the tiny infant at daycare. When the CEO returns to the van nine hours later, her baby is dead, and the daycare center never called to find out where the child was.

After reading this story on the air, I received a listener fax asking, "Do you think a parent has ever been playing with the children in the morning and 'forgotten' to go to work!?!?" *Brilliant* analogy! I know, I know . . . parenting your own children may seem like an outrageous notion in these times of casual divorce, promiscuous reproduction and geographical fragmentation of the family. But the facts show that these circumstances are a disaster to the lives and emotional well-being of children. Cheryl Gochnauer's *Stay-At-Home Handbook* is a survival guide, spiritual manual and how-to book for parents who are shifting their focus from career to family.

One of the most frequently asked questions on my radio show is "How can I become a stay-at-home-mom?" However, the more important question is, *Why* should I become a stay-at-home parent?

Cheryl answers both of these questions with humor, insight and a strong faith. She shares her personal story of transforming from an over-stressed, anxious working woman into a successful, nurturing, stay-at-home mom. This decision involves many more elements than simply giving up a job. *Stay-At-Home Handbook* discusses financial issues and also addresses the fears, insecurities and problems faced by stay-at-home moms. Additionally Cheryl expertly outlines the joys, fulfillment and pride of raising children in a morally sound and secure environment.

I am frequently asked, "What does your radio signature, 'I Am My Kid's Mom,' mean?" Simply, it is a statement of *my* ultimate responsibility and most important job—to be an active participant in my son's life. Cheryl Gochnauer is a shining example of how to parent without sacrificing your own unique, creative talents and abilities so you can proudly say, "I, too, am my kid's mom."

Dr. Laura Schlessinger

Introduction

Since you've picked this book up and started flipping through it, it's a safe bet that you're a parent. Not only that, I'd wager that you're devoted to your children, and you're looking for ways to maximize both the quality and quantity of your time with them.

You've come to the right place, and the right book. *Stay-at-Home Handbook* shares the experiences of a wide range of present and prospective at-home parents. Each chapter is self-contained, so you can read them in any order, starting with the topic closest to your heart. And the chapters are short enough to be read in a few minutes—perfect for the parent on the run.

It doesn't matter whether you're presently working full-time, part-time or are already an at-home parent. The key is your heart, your focus, your *determination* to rearrange your priorities so that nothing—no job, no bill, nobody—hinders you from building the best possible relationship with your spouse and your kids.

Tell me, Cheryl—what job, bill or person do I need to move out of the way?

I can't answer that. But by the time you finish reading this book, you'll have the tools to figure that out for yourself.

The answer will be different for the next person picking up this book. That's because you're unique. And so are your kids. Your situation is literally one in a billion.

But guess what? You won't be alone as you sort through your options, looking for the best fit for your family. Your Father walks right along with you, always willing to share his insights and empowerment. After all, he's totally devoted to his children too.

PART 1

Checking Your Attitude

*"Tell me another job
that rewards its workers
like at-home parenting does.
I'm talking about
concrete, life-changing,
soul-nourishing pay-offs."*

1

I Am Woman—
& Mommy Too

A valid career choice

*R*aise your hand if you still remember all the
words to Helen Reddy's testament to feminists everywhere, "I
Am Woman." Somewhere in my basement there's an old cas-
sette tape recording of me belting out those verses, a preteen
captivated with the idea of equality and getting ahead in this
world.

I roared through my twenties until I got hoarse, clutching to
the precepts of that seventies anthem. The world was wide
open, and I ran with the pack, putting as much mileage as possible between me and the dreaded kitchen sink. I got my college degree (one of the first women in my family to do so),
started a career and landed myself a progressively minded
husband. Together Terry and I settled into a frenetic pace,

each giving our best to our employers while eyeing the next goal: a better lifestyle, a new house, two comfortable 401(k) retirement plans.

I bought the line that as a liberated female, I could have it all. But soon after our first baby, Karen, was born, cracks began appearing in my New Woman philosophy.

Cracks began appearing in my New Woman philosophy.

Both baby and employer demanded my full attention, and only the elusive Super Woman could satisfy both masters. I had never met this Super Woman, of course, but often heard glowing reviews of her prowess. She remained my hero as I struggled to give 100 percent at work and 100 percent at home. (I think it's obvious that math has never been my strong point.) Things got more complicated when Carrie, the second Gochnauer heir, arrived, squalling for her piece of the pie.

As time passed, the phrase "Yes, I've paid the price, but look how much I've gained" began to take on a certain irony. No longer able to pay the full amount upfront, I had to broker credit terms both at work and at home.

To my child: "I know Wesley's mom got to come see him perform. I got to see you, too, honey. She made a video. Isn't that great? Well, I'm cheering now. Don't pout. All right. I'll see if I can get some comp time before the next _____ ." (Fill in the blank: game, play, contest, presentation and so on.)

To my boss: "I understand completely. The company's goals are my goals, and I want to give you my full support. But I won't be able to work over tonight. I don't have a sitter. How about this weekend? My kids are going to their grandma's."

Frowns. Everywhere I looked there were frowns. On my kids' faces. On my boss's face. In the mirror—yes, there was another one.

A Type A personality can take such rejection for only so long. Being an overachiever, I finally decided to take charge. Using a classic winning strategy, I picked one area in which to excel, and in this case it was with my children.

I decided to become a stay-at-home mom.

What a relief! The effects of this simplifying choice have transformed my life and the lives of every member of my family. No longer under the dictates of a Day-Timer, there is time to sort out priorities, to enjoy a gentler pace, to *live*.

I love it. So do Karen and Carrie. My boss—well, he will just have to get along without me for a while.

Terry is a different guy now too. He takes comfort in having a partner who is committed to renovating our once stressed-out home into a more peaceful haven. He knows his daughters, Karen and Carrie, receive the best possible care around the clock from the one woman who loves them, and him, the most.

Are finances tight? Yes. Is it worth it? You bet.

Are finances tight? Yes. Is it worth it? You bet. A peanut butter and jelly sandwich with my daughters in the park beats a croissant with a client any day.

Smiles. Everywhere I look, smiles. In the mirror—yes, there's another one.

If I have to, I can do anything . . . one thing at a time. I am strong. I am invincible. For this season of my life I am Mommy.

Homebodies Hint. Look at your life objectively. What is the role you most desire to play at this time in your life? Do you need to do some priority shuffling?

2

My Real Job

My home number is my work number

All I needed was a loaf of bread and a gallon of milk and I was out of there. Scribbling the amount, I tore out the check, simultaneously trying to keep my seven-year-old away from the magazine rack and my three-year-old out of the Starbursts.

"Work number?" asked the convenience store clerk.

"My phone number's on the check," I replied. "I'm a stay-at-home mom."

The clerk looked up. "Uh, Ma'am . . . I need a real work number."

Startled, I didn't know whether to cry, scream or melt into the linoleum as people behind me fidgeted. With one comment this young stranger stripped me of status and confidence, and unprepared for such a confrontation, I buckled.

I put my husband's number on the check.

Standing in a friend's kitchen later, I continued to sort out my humiliation over the incident. How could he treat me like that? If I had walked in a year earlier,

"Uh, Ma'am ... I need a real work number."

dressed in my power suit and armed with a phone number plus extension, I'd have passed muster. But somehow all the education, experience and respect obtained to this point in my life meant nothing because I no longer had a "real" job.

Glancing out the patio doors, a line flashed through my head: "I have found the Promised Land, and it's in my own backyard." Immediately I headed for my computer and tapped out a lengthy letter to the editor, asserting that deciding to become a stay-at-home mom was as valid a career choice as any other, and outlining the reasons why.

Now that I've been writing for newspapers for several years, I know that most articles run about four to five hundred words. I didn't know anything about the newspaper business then, however, and my heartfelt manifesto ran twenty-five hundred fiery words, every syllable screaming with passion. I marched into the local newspaper office and handed it to the editor in person. God bless that man: he started reading, nodded his head, and away we went.

That is how Homebodies, my online and print ministry for at-home parents, began. I wasn't a writer in my old life; I was an administrative worker. But this kid's actions lit me up. My livid letter to the editor ran as a four-part series, sparking a regular column, which spread to more newspapers and online parenting magazines, laying groundwork for my book *So You Want to Be a Stay-at-Home Mom,* which ignited the Homebodies

The Promised Land is in my own backyard.

website (www.homebodies.org), a Gospel Communications Network entity that now serves thousands of at-home parents each week, encouraging and empowering them in their chosen profession.

All because this guy wouldn't accept my home phone as a real work number. If I could remember which store it was, I would go back and thank him. Of course, with customer service like that, they're probably out of business by now.

Tell me another job that rewards its workers like at-home parenting does. I am talking about concrete, life-changing, soul-nourishing payoffs. As mothers we are the first line of defense for our children; we are also the window through which they view the world. Although some tasks can be tedious, keep on keeping on. "Every day that we repeat the same old routine, we are teaching our children diligence," says Merrie, who is raising her family in Blue Springs, Missouri. "Every time we read stacks of papers from school, we show our children that they are valuable. Every time we correct them or force them to pick up after themselves, we are teaching them character.

"Sometimes it is hard to see the forest for the trees, but try to think of what the alternative would be. No one else can be your kids' mom. No one else will have your specific set of values to instill in them, and no one else is as emotionally tied to their future as you are. It matters.

"What we do is so very worth the price we pay," Merrie concludes. "It's exhausting and can be mundane, but the rewards will be there for a job well done in the end."

Lori, an Illinois mom, posted this eloquent note online at the Homebodies forums: "My job here is important. So is your job, dear fellow stay-at-home mom. We are raising the future Christians, legislators, judges, inventors, thinkers, teachers, artists, preachers, evangelists, doctors, military personnel and statesmen of the world. How awesome is that? The hand that rocks the cradle *is* the hand that rules the world. Just because society has chosen to believe a lie doesn't mean we have to. The truth is still the truth: we're vitally important, and our lives have eternal meaning."

 Homebodies Hint. Write a formal job description for a successful at-home parent.

3

Don't Sweat It

Avoiding the "soaps & bonbons" caricature

Although I resist the notion that at-home parents wear nothing but sweats and spit-up, it is true that days can go by before I seriously consider what I look like to others. After all, there are more important things to dwell on than whether my sneakers match my shirt.

But there is something to be said for feeling presentable, and I am trying hard to not fall into the caricature of a slovenly stay-at-home mom.

"You know, that 'frumpy housewife' was a toughy for me," Shauna, a former Kansas City teacher, admits. "I was so glad to *not* have to be in hose and uncomfortable shoes that I went sweats and t-shirts all the time! Then I got tired of looking at myself being so sloppy."

Stephanie, who used to work as a human resources specialist, agrees. "Looking like the frumpy housewife is an easy trap to fall in, isn't it? I mean, who wants to feel like a stuffed sausage in panty hose when you don't need to!"

But the freedom of choosing your own wardrobe each day can backlash into poor self-esteem if you let your appearance totally slide.

> The freedom of choosing your wardrobe can backlash into poor self-esteem.

"I have always been afraid somebody will say, 'Look at her, she must be a stay-at-home mom,'" confesses Lori, who has been home about nine years.

"It's so important not to lose touch with the physical you," says J.J., who left her job in Springdale, Arkansas, to take care of her little boy. "I am not the type of person to forego the makeup or hair routine. I feel naked without perfume. I keep my toenails painted red! These things keep me connected to the 'me' before I became a mom."

Working out at the gym helps J.J. feel rejuvenated too. "I know this is not an affordable option for many stay-at-home parents, but when my husband got a raise recently, this was the thing we splurged on."

Rather than detracting from her family, J.J.'s time alone enhances her at-home experience. "I get to have a couple of hours to myself, shower, get dressed, have some 'girl time' in the locker room with other women and boost my self-esteem. I really feel good about myself when I leave. Then I am fresh and ready for a full day with my son!"

Kass runs an Arizona in-home business while raising her three sons. "Being not only a stay-at-home but a work-at-home mom, it's pretty important for me to be more than presentable when out and about. There's nothing like bumping into a potential customer and your hair is up on end, and you have baby spit-up on your shirt and holes in your jeans. Talk about embarrassing."

Stephanie refuses to look scruffy and laze around just because she doesn't work in a traditional office setting. Here are some things she does to maintain her sense of order and respect for herself.

"I have my desk at home set up just like it was at work. I even have my old nameplate, except I changed my title to read simply 'SAHM' [Stay-at-Home Mom]. I turn my computer on when I wake up, and I use my Outlook calendar to keep track of all of my tasks, appointments, preschool projects, church meetings and luncheon dates. It keeps me organized and eliminates a zillion sticky notes all over the house. My calendar is *full*.

"My day is very regimented. I have something going on all of the time, whether it be household chores or a special project. I'm busier now than I was when I was working, only in a different way.

"I try to wake up a half hour before my boys, grab a shower and get dressed. I do apply full makeup every day, put on my earrings and watch, wear perfume, cream my hands and curl my hair. My daughter is usually watching me during my makeup ritual and asks for red cheeks too.

"I honestly do not wear sweats ever, unless I'm tackling a messy project. My attire is usually a pair of pants (if jeans, they're not ratty and I press them so they look nice), a blouse or sweater and slip-on shoes.

"I try to maintain a healthy lifestyle and get plenty of rest so I don't look fatigued and harried. I think nothing beats frumpiness better than a stylish haircut. It's the first thing people see, and if your hair looks tired, so do you. I dress my children in clean, neat, but functional clothes as well. I believe that my family's appearance is a reflection of me, so they should look nice too."

In her Idaho home Angela is convinced that whether at school, business or home, dress affects attitude. "I go through the whole getting-ready thing every day, even if we're not going anywhere. I feel more put together and seem to accomplish more."

Angela also defies the couch potato syndrome. "When I first became a stay-at-home mom, I did watch some TV. I think I was in the vacation phase; you're so excited to be home and trying to find your routine. I would schedule my newborn's feeding time around 11:00 so I could watch Matlock!

Defy couch potato syndrome.

"That quickly grew old and now I never turn the thing on, except to catch Oprah once every few weeks. There's just too much to do. If you really look at your home and family, there is always something that you can be doing. Not that down time isn't necessary (goodness knows it is), but I didn't want TV to be a regular part of my day. I would end up feeling like I had just wasted an hour or more."

There's nothing wrong with being laid back. On rainy, blustery days my warm fleece pants and pullover are heavenly. And it's not unusual for me to skip the Clinique and simply face the world with a soap-and-water shine.

To help maintain my positive self-esteem, however, I'll be keeping the sweats and lounging to a minimum. Don't touch my bonbons though. I'm holding on to my chocolate until I die!

Homebodies Hint. Consider simple steps you can take to spruce up your physical image, such as getting more sleep, wearing makeup, dabbing on some perfume. Do these things to help you feel better about yourself, rather than to impress others.

4

There's Snow Place Like Home

No more school cancellation woes

*B*lue Springs Elementary ... Lee's Summit R-9 ... Grandview High . . . Community Christian School." The announcer confirmed what I suspected when I peeked out the blinds at dawn and spotted the thick blanket of snow. There would be no school today.

With a whispered, "Yes!" I turned off the TV and jumped back in bed. Snuggling deeper under the covers, I savored yet another benefit to being a stay-at-home mom: I didn't have to get out in that wintry mess! Instead I anticipated a day of hot chocolate and games with the girls. But first, another blissful hour of sleep.

A tiny set of tiger house shoes padded across the carpet. With a sleepy half-grin, Carrie burrowed her way under the comforter, tossed and turned a couple of times, and then gently snored. My own eyes fluttered shut as I remembered . . .

When I worked full-time, a school closing announcement had a much different effect on our family. Instead of tranquility, the house roared with frantic Plan Bs.

Hopefully a backup sitter could be arranged without too much trouble. But I hated taking the kids out in frigid cold, even after bundling them up like mummies.

Then there was the drive, or should I say crawl, to work. Hadn't any of these people seen snow before? Worse were the reckless drivers using the shoulder as another lane, scowling at wimps maneuvering ice at under eighty miles per hour.

I approached hills and stop signs with apprehension, as the dashboard radio churned out accident reports. By the time I reached the office, I had to pry my clenched fingers off the steering wheel.

Exiting the building nine hours later, I joined the throng of frozen-breathed coworkers scraping ice off windows and dislodging gunk from wiper blades. Inching out of the slippery parking lot, I passed whining, spinning tires and men jogging for jumper cables.

Reaching the interstate, I again switched on the radio. Everything was backed up. Interchanges were clogged. Alternate routes were jammed too.

Glancing at the clock, my stomach churned. I visualized the sitter, arms crossed and determined to charge me a mint for arriving past six o'clock. At this rate I wouldn't get home until eight.

A light appeared on the dash. "Low fuel." It was a nightmare.

And as I awakened, I realized it really *was* a nightmare. I had been dreaming, my extra hour of sleep spent spinning old tapes.

Karen stirred in the other room. A few moments later she was under my comforter too, unwilling to let Carrie monopolize mom. Wrapping an arm around each of my babies, I smiled.

Rain, sleet or snow, I love being a stay-at-home mom. The pressure to be somewhere at a certain time, no matter what the weather conditions, is off. No sitter is waiting for us; no boss is eyeing the clock. If it's bad out, the Gochnauer girls stay in.

Rain, sleet or snow, I love being a stay-at-home mom.

I wish we could keep Terry here with us. (First, I have to figure out how my truck-driving husband can make his deliveries from home!) At least I can fill him with warm coffee and prayers before he hits the icy roads. The upside is, Terry can do his own traveling without worrying about members of his family getting stranded somewhere.

Meanwhile the girls are stretching and ready to rise. The accumulating snow beckons, and a search commences for snowsuits that fit. Sorting through our garage sale treasures, we pull out thirty-dollar ski overalls that I picked up for a dollar at a garage sale last summer. House shoes traded for Winnie the Pooh boots, my daughters hit the drifts outside our front door.

The snow is pristine, since most of the neighbor kids slid off to daycare before they had a chance to play. I watch Karen and Carrie from inside the glass storm door, sledding down the side yard and pummeling each other with snowballs. Before long, they are shivering in the foyer, red-faced and teeth chattering, kicking off boots and piling wet snowsuits, caps, scarves and mittens on the linoleum.

It's a mess, but it's for a good cause. I'll take a load to the dryer while the girls scuffle over which video to watch.

No school means no homework—at least for the day. The movie starts as I heat the hot chocolate and marshmallows. Each of us grabs a blanket and heads for the couch, ready to curl up together and enjoy some unplanned quality time.

The weather outside may be frightful, but my home is so delightful.

The weather outside may be frightful, but my home is so delightful. And because we've no place to go, let it snow, let it snow, let it snow!

Homebodies Hint. If you're an at-home mom, preserve some memories of past snow days by writing down your experiences. If you're working outside the home, give some thought as to how you would use snow days if you were free to enjoy them with your little ones.

5

Beyond
"Ma-Ma" & "Goo"

Feeling appreciated

As working mothers, we had bosses to reward us and coworkers to share our workplace successes. Now that we have exchanged our cubicles for our living rooms, affirmation is harder to come by. This is especially true when our children are still in their cribs, are toddlers or simply haven't grasped the fine art of thanking mom for all she does for them.

"I have had the most pitiful last couple of days, and by this morning, was shrouded in self-pity," says Merrie. "None of my children seem to respect me. All the housework that I had accomplished had been undone by a toddler demolition crew, and we were all a little testy because of fighting off head colds.

"My head was splitting as I drove the kids to school. Then I had to wait in line at the bank twenty-five minutes. All the while, my three-year-old was screaming.

"We continued our morning shopping, aspirin helped the headache, and things began looking better. Stores were absolutely jammed, but I found some good bargains," Merrie says. "My little tyrant cooled her heels just long enough for me to pick up a few things, and we headed home after a run through McDonald's.

Most kids haven't grasped the fine art of thanking mom for all she does.

"Once home she peeled her winter clothing off for the twentieth time that day and insisted on a sheer, glittery dance outfit. As I fumbled with pulling up the sequined confection, I irritably glanced at her face and it happened: one of those magic moments that make everything else fall into perspective. Pink sequins set off her more-strawberry-than-blonde hair and enormous blue eyes looking into mine.

"She whispered, 'Dance with me, Mommy.'

"I slipped Nat King Cole into the CD player, and we swept along to 'Unforgettable.' I could tell she felt beautiful and cherished. I did too. By the time Nat King Cole was crooning 'Mona Lisa,' we were nose to nose in the rocking chair, sharing butterfly kisses."

Alas, it was not to last. "A few songs later, I discovered she was trying to pick leaves off the fichus tree behind my head," Merrie laughs. "Unbelievably, the song 'Straighten up and Fly Right' had just begun.

"The magic ended when the song did, as my daughter slithered off my lap in search of more mischievous endeavors. Okay, it's nap time!"

Precious moments such as Merrie described are often sandwiched between harried challenges. Don't forget to stay alert for the unexpected light in the midst of the tunnel. Sometimes we get so busy we miss these nuggets of parenting joy that are so important in affirming us as mothers.

"When you cuddle your toddler after a fall or a nightmare, and their arms go around your neck, you can feel the appreciation," says Kathi, an Oklahoma mom of five. "Maybe they don't have words, but they have love. Love knows no age restraint. They love me unconditionally, even when I've had a bad day or burned the toast."

"My husband gives me a lot of affirmation," Shauna points out. "Whenever I'm having one of those 'underpaid maid' days, he reminds me that my job is most important, and that our boys—when they realize that I made the choice to be home with them and gave them my first and best—will be overcome with appreciation!"

> They love me unconditionally, even when I've burned the toast.

In his job, Shauna's husband, Tom, works with daycare centers. "He thinks of our kids, warm and snuggled at home, having the privilege of playing in their own yard, napping in their own beds, reading books with their own mom, and getting to be a laid-back-all-around kid, instead of being shuffled through daycare for eight to twelve hours a day."

What about the times we're depressed and our husbands aren't around to encourage us?

"As moms, we all have down days, no matter how old our children are," acknowledges Terri, who is raising Katie and Austin in Claremont, New Hampshire. So Terri created an "I'm Special" box and filled it with thank you cards, birthday wishes, letters, cards and pictures made by her children. "It could be a box or basket, your personal choice. I've also included a candle, pictures of my family, a special candy or treat and a Bible.

"Everything is bundled up and put together. When I feel

blue, I pull them out, open a sunny window, light my candle and sift through all the cards and letters and reread them. I look at my family photos and pictures the kids have drawn, and soon I'm lifted again.

"Each day we touch someone's life, and I think we have to remind ourselves of this," Terri says. "We are all uniquely special as mothers. God knew what he was doing when he gave me my two children. He gave me my life!"

As you read this chapter, I bet you're thinking of your own special moments—those times when you've connected heart to heart with your child. Don't let those memories get away. You'll need them on the days when you're *not* connecting—like when your toddler is pounding her fists on the floor and you're wondering if your boss will take you back.

You *are* appreciated. You are doing a good job. You are special and unique. You are a hands-on parent, and that's a precious thing in the eyes of your child, your husband and your Lord.

Homebodies Hint. After hugging your children and thanking your husband for his encouragement and support of your at-home decision, compile your own "I'm Special" box. Fill it with things that will reaffirm you when the blues hit.

6

Savoring the Stay-at-Home Season

Rain or shine— seize your parenting day!

*A*s a kid, I could hardly wait to be grown up. Adults had money, could drive and didn't have to listen to their parents.

As a single adult, I could hardly wait to meet my future spouse. Married people had security, houses and were never lonely again.

As a wife, I could hardly wait to have children. Parents had wisdom, influence and somebody who looked just like them.

As a working mother, I could hardly wait to become a stay-at-home mom. Stay-at-home moms had clean houses, perfect children and quality time overflowing.

Now I'm a grownup, married, stay-at-home parent. I can

drive but still don't have much money. I'm a wife, but after watching friends grind through the divorce mill, I have learned vows don't guarantee security or hedge against loneliness. And though I've got two children, there are times I feel neither wise nor influential. At least with their flaming red hair, they do look somewhat like me.

> Our sense of purpose has to be greater than the mundane chores.

Finally, I am a stay-at-home mom, but still find a clean house and quality time elusive.

I could get discouraged about all this, but I choose instead to look at the positives. At each crossroads I've had the opportunity to make choices. I chose to go to college, to pursue a career, to marry my husband, to bear my children.

I also chose to become a stay-at-home mom. Like every other season I've lived through, there are days when it is tough.

"I think our sense of purpose has to be greater than the mundane chores," J.J. says. "The laundry in and of itself doesn't define me as a stay-at-home mom.

"God has given us the incredible opportunity to shape and mold our children. Although I am swimming in loads of dirty laundry, I don't see my purpose as simply keeping a clean house. It is very easy to get lost in the repetitive tasks we do every day. I try my best to keep it all in perspective.

"My goals are directed towards raising a happy, God-loving, self-respecting and well-rounded person, being active in my marriage, and creating a warm, comfortable home for my family and anyone who visits.

"These are not simple tasks," she acknowledges. "I will be spending the rest of my life trying to accomplish them. But right now I have the opportunity to focus my attention on these areas. Hopefully I am building a strong foundation for the future of my family. Someone once said that the purpose of all success in life is to be happy at home. How true!"

Angela recently reviewed prayer journals she had written when she first became a stay-at-home mom. "I was brand new to this, and the monotony of doing the same things day in and day out, only to have to start over the next day, was really wearing me down.

"I remember crying out to the Lord one day and asking, 'Is this really all you have for me? Is this how I am to spend the rest of my life, being a homemaker?' It was at that very moment that it hit me: exactly what the word *homemaker* means. It means that I am making a home, creating a haven for my family.

"Where would our families be if we didn't do the things we do for them? These are the things that make them feel safe, secure and loved; the things that make our husbands feel they can't wait to come home.

"That moment changed my whole thinking and how I viewed my calling in life."

When the baby is screaming and your toddler has smeared the dog with toothpaste, it can be tempting to recall quiet days in your cubicle at work. At least that's the way I like to remember them. It is easy to forget demanding bosses and pressure-cooking office politics. Or peeling a wailing child off my leg at daycare. Or scrapping with my spouse on a regular basis because frantic schedules left us each frayed and irritable.

My stay-at-home dream house isn't picture-perfect, but it's where I've chosen to be.

No, thanks. Sure, my stay-at-home dream house isn't always picture-perfect, but it's where I've chosen to be for this stage of our lives. So I accept the inevitable downtimes because I truly appreciate the good days. And on the whole, there are lots more days I feel like Pooh ("Yummy—honey!") than Eeyore ("Bah—bees!").

We've all heard it said that the years when our children are young zip by. That has certainly been true in my situation. I blinked after my first baby's birth, and six years were gone— spent nurturing my boss instead of my family. Another six have passed since I've been home. The second six were better than the first—even with the challenges that go hand-in-hand with the at-home experience. I was in the right place at the right time.

Stormy or fair, I'm savoring this SAHM season.

Homebodies Hint. Think of some challenges you are currently facing as an at-home parent, then find a positive that offsets each of the perceived negatives.

7

Put Mom
in Time-Out

Reserving quality time
for yourself

I believe every stay-at-home mom should be put in time-out at least once a week.

You heard me. She needs time out—of the house.

Get the poor woman outta there! If you don't, you're taking a horrible risk. Maintain an unrelenting parenting stance and this wonderful, family-focused woman is sure to morph into a fire-breathing, maxed-out mom. And we can't have that.

Granted, getting some of these dedicated ladies to take a even a short break can be challenging. "Oh, I just don't think that would be right," they protest, as their world swirls around them. "My kids will think I don't like them, and my husband will accuse me of goofing off."

On the contrary. Both your kids and your husband will benefit if you carve out some time for yourself. Time when you're obligation-free. Time when you pamper yourself. After all, the whole family needs to be nurtured, and that includes you. It helps no one if you pour your entire being into taking care of everyone else, and leave yourself a hollowed-out mess.

> We don't expect our husbands to work twenty-four hours a day.

We don't expect our husbands to work at their jobs twenty-four hours a day, seven days a week. In fact, wives usually resent spouses who do that. But if she's not careful, an over-amped, stay-at-home mom can easily find herself working around the clock, attempting to meet her family's every imagined wish and need.

You can't give if there is nothing to draw from. You are overdue for an emotional fill-up. But how do you go about soaking up some mommy time so you can get rejuvenated?

First of all, don't try this at home. Sure, you can grab the latest Tom Hanks/Meg Ryan video and some microwave popcorn and head for the TV/VCR combo in your bedroom, securing the door behind you. But I guarantee you won't even be through the opening credits before you will hear your husband off in the distance, making a major parenting mistake.

You whip open the door. "No, Babe; the red shirt does *not* go with the pink pants. Plus, Joey needs to wear a heavier jacket if you're taking them outside." You close the door firmly, locking it.

You just sprung Pandora's box, of course. Before you have a chance to settle back down with Tom and Meg, little fingers are wiggling under the door, punctuated by heavy toddler breathing and faint "whatcha doings"?

Get out of the house!

What do you do once you're out? It's a big world out there; choose anything unrelated to kids or housework. That means no errand running, appointment keeping or grocery shopping. Don't go anywhere near an M.D., IGA, CPA or Toys "R" Us.

Instead, allow your imagination to whisk you away to your favorite grown-up play zone.

Spend some time with your girlfriends, especially those without children. Take an evening college course that challenges you or an easy hands-on workshop that sparks your creativity. In the mood for a movie? Buy a ticket to a film you have been dying to see, preferably one without animated characters. Go to a favorite restaurant and order something slathered with onions, green peppers, hot sauce or anything else your kids think is disgusting. Swim in the deep end; rollerblade minus the antiseptic and Band-Aids; hike without anyone complaining about bugs. Hop in the front seat of the roller coaster and scream all the way down.

Are you in a shopping mood? Hey, I may not have much money, but I still like to look. And if I do happen to have a few extra dollars in my pocket, it's nice to try on outfits without my kids either draped over my feet, peeking under the changing stall or somersaulting down the next aisle.

Short on cash? Roll the minivan windows down, and go for a stress-free drive in the fresh-scented country, with a soft drink you don't have to share in your hand. Visit a bookstore or library sometime other than story hour; find a chair and read without interruption. Go to a park. Sit by a lake.

Feeling refreshed? Great! Now you can head back home and truly enjoy your family. You will, you know. You'll marvel at how lots of those things that were irritating you about your children are actually kinda cute.

Homebodies Hint. Talk with your spouse about building a guilt-free break into each week. Brainstorm some activities you would like to pursue, call your friends and mark two months of "Mom's Night Out" dates on the calendar.

8

Disarming
the Mommy Wars

Minimizing conflict between working & stay-at-home moms

I n case you haven't noticed, it is not unusual to run into friction between working and stay-at-home mothers. Listen closely: you can almost hear the schoolyardlike taunting: "I'm a better mommy than you are . . . nah, nah."

The "better mommy" ideal translates differently, according to which side of the working mom/stay-at-home mom issue a competitive parent happens to be on. Colleen encountered the wall at her husband's office Christmas party. Her husband helped her with her coat, then stepped away to greet some male coworkers. A couple of young women came up to Colleen and introductions began, along with the inevitable "What do you do?" question. When she answered, "I stay home with my kids," she was greeted with an awkward pause.

The conversation then switched to what everyone was getting their kids for Christmas. Trendy toys and pricey labels topped the lists, until it was Colleen's turn to share. She confidently told them about the handmade outfits she'd prepared, and the chill was complete. She could almost read their minds: "If she would get a job, she wouldn't have to give her kids cheap stuff."

Did I love my kids less when I was working? No!

Joanne ran into a reversed prejudice at a room parents' meeting one evening. She had been working a lot of required overtime, so this was the first gathering she had been able to attend.

As Joanne listened to ideas for an upcoming classroom party, she could see that a core group of stay-at-home moms was controlling the conversation. All the children's parties were scheduled during the day; treats and prizes were handmade. Joanne suddenly felt intimidated and out of place. She knew she couldn't get off work for the parties, and she didn't know when she'd have the time to bake cookies.

When Joanne suggested bringing store-bought pastries, she was told the idea had already been voted down at the last planning meeting. "Oh, that's right. You had to work."

Their attitudes said it all: "Go back to your office, Lady. We'll take it from here."

Unfortunately radical women fighting the Mommy Wars have successfully integrated distorted images of the opposing sides into our culture. We have no trouble conjuring up the caricatures: at-home moms as sloppy, bonbon-munching couch potatoes who couldn't make it in the real world, and working moms as money-hungry power brokers who trade their kids for things.

Whew—my blood pressure rises just reading that last paragraph! I guess that's because I have been both a working mom and an at-home parent, and neither of those awful images ever fit me. Well, okay; I admit I do enjoy the occasional bonbon. But I liked to snarf them when I was in the office too.

Before we start slinging accusations at each other, let's back things up a little. I was a working mom for six years. Recently I marked six years as a stay-at-home mom, so I can honestly say my parenting years have been split fifty-fifty. Did I love my kids any less when I was working a full-time job? You wanna duke it out? My job status has nothing to do with how I feel about my girls. So I say we stop firing the "I care more about my kids than you do" missiles right now.

Career flexibility is an empowerment issue, not a character issue. Moms now have the freedom and responsibility that comes with having more work options than at any other time in history: full time or part time; in the office or telecommuting; nights, days or split shifts; job-share or start your own business. Another valid career choice: become an at-home parent.

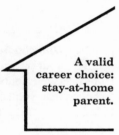

A valid career choice: stay-at-home parent.

The key is to find your niche. Personally, trying to work forty-plus hours a week while also striving to give my best to my husband and girls wiped me out physically and emotionally. By the time I let go of work to become a full-time mom, everyone could smell the smoke of my impending burnout. Coming home was the best thing I ever did.

But that's me. There are other women who flourish in the accelerated lifestyle of a working mom. The fast pace invigorates them.

Whether working full time, part time or as a stay-at-home mom, you must have the support of your individual family. If a woman feels called to work, and her children are thriving on the amount of time she is able to spend with them, she deserves our respect. Who am I to say they would all be happier if she was a stay-at-home mom? The at-home lifestyle has been a blessing to me, but may not be the best choice for her.

Likewise, a woman called to be home with her children should be esteemed. A society that values at-home parents, both male and female, is long overdue.

Let's set aside the tug-of-war and acknowledge that a woman's place is wherever God calls her. Declare a cease-fire in the Mommy Wars, and enjoy the resulting peacetime alliances.

Homebodies Hint. What can you do to deflect criticism of your present or proposed stay-at-home status? Do you have any preconceived notions about parents who have made different work choices than you have?

9

So What Do You Do?

Bucking the "nonworking" stereotype

Like most at-home parents, I haven't had a bonbon since February, and the only soaps I watch are floating in my kids' bubble baths. So why do these myths about stay-at-home moms persist?

In a world that regularly spotlights and condemns prejudice, homemakers continue to be targeted as less driven, less productive and less intelligent.

"I have had several people say things like, 'I guess it was too hard for you to juggle work and kids' or 'Why would you give up a career for kids?'" says Michelle, a stay-at-home mom from Missouri. A former employer was even harsher. "'Well, I won't hire you back. If you quit to stay home and do nothing, then why would I want you here?' I was stunned by that," Michelle

The only soaps I watch are floating in my kids' bubble baths.

remembers. "I can't believe he thought taking care of my children was doing nothing."

Joan, whose son was about a year old at the time, was chatting with neighbors at a block party. "Another neighbor, who knows me very well, and his wife, 'Susie-Q,' were talking to me about their kids, who were one and two and a half," Joan says. "They were raving about their daycare center, and Mr. Neighbor said, 'You know, even if Susie-Q stayed home with the kids, I'd really want to send Junior there a few days a week. He's already learned his colors, and letters, and everything.' As if a stay-at-home mom can't teach those things even better one-on-one!"

Stories like these make me laugh, yell or cry, depending on my mood. But one thing remains consistent: Although my focus has changed, my basic personality has not. No one can take away the education or experiences that have molded me into the person I am today. I may wear jeans more often than business suits, but don't let the clothes fool you.

I *work* as an at-home parent, and I take my job very seriously.

Many at-home moms feel great about their decision to focus on family, until they run into a carbon copy of their former working self.

"So, what do you do?"

That simple question can set off a flurry of conflicting emotions. In an attempt to validate their choice, some moms reach for lofty-sounding titles like domestic engineer. Others suddenly feel self-conscious and downplay their role: "I'm just a housewife." Unfortunately no matter how they answer, too many at-home mothers are rewarded with a blank look and change of subject.

Racism is no longer tolerated. Diversity in a variety of areas is valued and even demanded. No one is looking to set women's rights back thirty years. But if we are going to promote diversity, let that openness extend to our sisters who have chosen to nurture their children first and their careers second.

"In my social circle it was not accepted for the wives to stay at home," says Lori. "It still isn't accepted. So I changed circles.

"I love staying at home. My husband is a wonderful provider and is my staunchest supporter. For me, coming home is the best thing I have ever done. I thank God that he allowed me this great privilege and awesome honor, even if the world doesn't agree."

> In my social circle, staying home was not accepted. So I changed circles.

"I'm starting on my fifth year as a stay-at-home mom, and I've come to realize a few things," observes Beverly, who has children in both elementary school and college. "We still haven't starved to death, we aren't naked, and we don't live in a washing machine box on the side of the road because I quit my job.

"Since I have more time to spend with my kids, my seven-year-old can read beyond the level of his peers. I'm able to go on all the school field trips, and I can help in the classroom as much as I want, which helps me get in good with the teachers. I've discovered my college-age child needs me at home just as much as a child in elementary school."

And to top it off, Beverly says, "I'm not a nonproductive member of society."

"Hey, here's the reality," Shauna asserts. "We *all* work.

Some work in the home full time, some out of the home full time and some out of the home part time. I've done it all three ways: taught school full time for five years, part time one year, and I've now been home full time for two years. The mix that works for us as individuals and for our families is as unique as we are. We should never make each other feel badly for making decisions for our own families."

Even as we anticipate the day when at-home mothers are valued as much as other working women, let's always remember that confidence begins within. If you know you have made the right choice for you and your family, then it doesn't matter what anyone else thinks or says. Whether confronted with a remote-clicking caricature or a census form that categorizes at-home mothers as "nonworking," you know that you're performing one of the most important jobs in the world. So the next time someone asks, "What do you do?" you can respond that you're working to make this world a better place, one life at a time.

Homebodies Hint. It can be easier to handle situations when we prepare for them in advance. What will you say the next time someone asks, "So, what do you do?"

PART 2

Managing
Your Money

*"I like new things as much as the next person,
but since I decided to become an
at-home parent,
I know I can't have everything at once.
That doesn't mean I can't have
anything at all.
It simply means I have to be
more creative than just whipping out
my credit card
when I want to purchase something."*

10

Pride of the Penny Pinchers

Using coupons, rebates & other discounts

What kind of image leaps to mind when you think of a frugal person? Narrow eyes darting across price tags? Tight lips tallying up purchases? Gnarled knuckles squeezing the blood out of a quarter?

A truly frugal person doesn't look this way at all. Instead her sharp eyes catch the bargain on the sales rack, she smiles as she goes over her receipt, and she knows where she can splurge, because she has fashioned her budget to be a guide to, not a padlock on, her spending habits.

"Staying home and living on one income has opened my eyes up," says J.J. "I have a whole new respect for money that I didn't have before. I honestly had no idea how little we could live on. I'm ashamed to admit it, but I used to spend my whole paycheck every two weeks when I worked outside the home. My husband paid the bills and I shopped. And we still managed to rack up debt! How crazy is that?"

As J.J. points out, most couples are adept at spending whatever they have available. Remember that last raise your spouse got, and how it was going to help you breathe easier financially? It is amazing how quickly the extra money gets eaten up by "necessities" like new clothes, bigger cars and nicer houses. A common trap is charging items on credit cards, anticipating paying them off when the windfall arrives. But by then the newness of the purchases has worn off, and it isn't any fun to simply pay bills. We'll think about that tomorrow. Today let's party!

Simply deferring a purchase can often move it from the "must have" category into the "maybe later" column. Carrie, who keeps a close eye on her Delaware family's budget, remembers some great advice she heard growing up. "My aunt told me when I was a little girl that if you go shopping and see something you think you really want, walk away from it. If in a week it is still on your mind, then go buy it. Most likely you won't be thinking about it at all, or will have already decided that you don't really need that item. It really works for me."

I like new things as much as the next person, but since I decided to become an at-home parent, I know I can't have everything at once. That doesn't mean I can't have anything at all. It simply means I have to be more creative than just whipping out my credit card when I want to purchase something.

A favorite Bible passage of mine is James 4:2, which says, "You do not have, because you do not ask." This verse speaks directly to anyone on a tight budget. Instead of saying, "We're poor; there's no way we can afford that," start looking at your options for slashing the cost of items you need.

Since coming home, I have been able to trim my family's budget by one thousand dollars a month, not including the $960 monthly daycare costs we saved when I quit my job. How did I do it? You'd be surprised how many miserly measures a determined mom can discover. Every dollar I save is a dollar I don't have to work outside the home to earn. Here are some steps to consider as you bring your own spending into line.

> Every dollar I save is a dollar I don't have to work outside the home to earn.

Housing costs. Have you got the best mortgage interest rate available? If not, consider refinancing, especially if you qualify for one of those "no-cost" loans that roll closing costs into the loan amount. Terry and I did that and lowered our monthly payment by $150 with no out-of-pocket expenses.

Summer cooling and winter heating bills are potential budget busters. Contact your utility companies to see if they offer level payment plans. That way, no matter what your actual usage is, your bill remains about the same each month.

For home maintenance learn to make repairs yourself or barter with friends who possess those skills.

Communication costs. Take a hard look at any home-based electronic subscription services. Do you need a paid messaging service (like caller ID or Call Notes), or will an answering machine work as well? If you have a second phone line for your computer, try cutting back to one and use a free online phone service to alert you to incoming calls while you're surfing the Net.

Could a free Internet service provider meet your Web needs? Free ISPs usually run a small advertising banner while you're online, but many people put up with that to save over two hundred dollars a year.

Can you reduce your long distance phone bill by either switching providers or making calls on your mobile phone? Many mobile phone plans include free long distance. For that matter, do you need a mobile phone? Consider using e-mail in place of long distance or postage whenever possible.

Does your family watch all two hundred cable or satellite channels you've signed up for? Or could they be content with the basic package, or even free network TV?

Speaking of subscriptions, if your local newspaper has a website, read the news online. I still buy my Sunday paper, but only because it contains coupons and sales flyers. That issue pays for itself.

Credit card costs. Are you dating your credit cards? Do you take them out to eat, to the movies and other fun places, and lavish them with expensive finance charges and late fees? It is time to break up. Keep one all-purpose card (MasterCard, VISA and so on) for emergencies (stashed somewhere other than your wallet) and cut up all the others. Make sure the one card you've chosen has the best rate available to you, with no annual fee.

Consider rolling all your outstanding installment loans (college, furniture, car and so on) into one tax-deductible home equity loan. Shop around for the best interest, then ask your preferred lender to match the rate. Important: Only use home equity loans if you're committed to paying off your debt. If you default on a car loan, you lose your car. But if you default on a home equity loan, you lose your house.

Automotive costs. When I was working, I had a nice car—a new, power-everything, look-at-me-I'm-successful automobile. I admit it. I looked *good* in that car.

But the extravagant monthly payment was standing between me and my kids. What's the use of a great car if it's just parked in the lot at work? I'd rather have a paid-off vehicle I can pile my kids into on a bright, sunny weekday afternoon and drive to the park, zoo or playground.

Afraid of selling your new car to buy an older model that may need repairs? An imaginary four-hundred-dollar bill on an

> Extravagant bills stood between me and my kids.

older, paid-off car beats a real four-hundred-dollar payment each and every month.

Another benefit to driving an older car: lower insurance rates. Plus if it's paid off, usually only liability coverage is required. Check into discounts that may be available once you're not driving back and forth to work every day.

No matter what kind of insurance you purchase—auto, home, health—reduce your monthly premium by choosing the highest deductible you feel comfortable with. Also see if your provider gives discounts if you list more than one policy with them.

Grocery and retail store costs. Retailers know shoppers love good buys. That's why they consistently offer special promotions, coupons and rebates on everything from cereal to cars. Such perceived bargains draw buyers into the showrooms and the supermarkets, ready to claim their slice of the savings.

Retailers also know that when everything is said and done, only a small fraction will follow through and claim the complicated discount offers that initially enticed them. So they make the cost cutting options available, knowing their loss exposure is minimal.

Why don't people pick up the free money represented by special promotions, coupons and rebates? Some fall for the bait and switch. "We just sold the last one; but this other item, though a little more expensive, is a great value." (If this happens to you, leave the store immediately. You are dealing with crooks.) Know exactly which item you came in to see, right down to the model number. If they don't have it on hand, ask them to call a sister store and have one sent over, or have them hold it for pickup.

Others forget their coupons, or don't maximize their worth. For instance, a forty-cent coupon is worth eighty cents if you shop at a store that doubles coupons. That's a 100 percent increase in value, obtained by simply choosing one store over another. Be sure to compare prices, however, to make sure the double-coupon store isn't charging more overall for their products, thereby reducing your savings.

Then there are the rebates, which usually represent the biggest savings of all. They also pose the biggest hassle, but are worth it if you simply follow through. Hold on to your receipts; you'll need to send in either a copy or the original. (You should be holding onto receipts anyway, ready to take stores up on their price matching guarantees if an item you bought goes on sale within thirty days.) Cut the UPC codes from boxes before you throw them away. And stash the rebate forms in your pocketbook like cash, which is what they represent.

Follow the directions on the rebate form to the smallest detail. Some companies try to wear you down by making the process as convoluted as possible. Outlast them and pocket the savings for your family.

Some of the best buys are combos of sale plus coupon plus rebate.

The best buys happen when you come across those great combinations of sale plus coupon plus rebate. It is conceivable that you will walk away from the transaction with a free product, plus change in your pocket, even after slapping a stamp on the rebate envelope. These are the times I wear my penny pincher label with pride.

Entertainment costs. What's the key element in any date? The people involved, of course. Although it's fun to splurge every once in a while, an activity doesn't have to be expensive to be memorable.

Play charades, blow bubbles, go bike-riding or rollerblading. Take tots to story time at the library or local bookstore. Use candles at supper, or involve neighbors in a progressive dinner, sampling different courses and cuisine at each house. Draw movie marquee posters advertising tonight's video. Fill up a collapsible pool, turn on the sprinkler, grab squirt guns and water balloons . . . you get the picture. All these ideas are virtually free and definitely entertaining, especially if you're in control of the Super Soaker.

> I wear my Penny Pincher label with pride.

"I still love to shop," Carrie says, "but I get that 'rush' now in different ways: hearing the clerk at the grocery store telling me my new total after he has subtracted my coupons from the original bill, finding brand-new looking Carters overalls at a resale shop for $6, catching errors on my phone statement. You get the point!"

Yes, I do. Let's all strive for the rush of being the best stewards we can, no matter how much money we have to work with.

Homebodies Hint. Grab your spouse and go on your own treasure hunt, discovering spots in your budget where you can eke out savings. What are some spending strategies you can take to leave more money in your wallet?

11

Hark, the Herald
Registers Ring

Gift giving on a budget

Q*uick—tell me what you bought* your in-laws
for Christmas last year. While you're working on that, tell me
what they gave you.

Can't remember? Let's see. There's that sweater I like . . .
wait, I picked that up myself when I returned the battery-
operated whisk broom Aunt Sally sent.

Hmmm. It's usually a book or something. Nope, it doesn't
jingle a bell. I give up.

This Christmas I am determined to give gifts that will be
remembered past New Year's Eve. The retailers are more than
willing to help us with our shopping. On the limited budget of
a stay-at-home mom, however, discovering special presents
becomes a bit challenging, so planning is critical.

A good guideline is to keep each person's personality and hobbies in mind, then build frugal gift choices around their interests. We also want to avoid the January, 21-percent APR finance charge blues, so here are some ideas to keep us from overspending too.

Set a budget. Compile a list of people you will be buying gifts for and decide how much you're going to spend. Stick to your budget, purchasing only what you can afford. If you do use credit, remember that any sales prices will probably be offset by finance charges. Instead of pulling out plastic, use cash religiously.

Use cash religiously.

Use coupons and rebates, and shop sales. Comparison shop by sifting through ad fliers and calling different stores. As the old jingle goes, let your fingers do the walking to save gas and time. Found what you want? Get all the details: price, model number, color. Then call your favorite store close to home and see if they'll price-match the other retailer.

Watch your totals. If you shop online, don't forget to add in shipping costs. Writing checks or using check cards? Keep all receipts in one place in your purse or wallet and immediately update your check register so you don't lose track of what you've spent. Another reason to keep receipts: thirty-day price guarantees. If an item goes on sale before Christmas, ask for a refund.

Shopping for children. Younger children usually appreciate several small gifts more than one big one. They also count to see how many packages their siblings are getting, so no matter how much money you have, balance the number of gifts as well as the amount spent on each child.

Buying for your spouse. I have been married almost twenty

years. The first ten years I hoped my husband would get me something romantic. Instead I consistently received "man gifts": steak knives, hand vacs, my own fishing pole. Years eleven through fifteen I dropped heavy hints: "I love things that make me feel pretty," "Ooooh, look at that scarf!" and "This perfume smells wonderful." I still ended up with fireplace tools and car accessories.

The past four years I have asked for *exactly* what I want, providing brand name, size, color—everything but written directions to the store. Christmas morning may not be a surprise, but I sure love my gifts, and my hubby is happy that I'm happy. Plus he hasn't wasted a lot of money.

If you're not sure what to get your mate, hand them a catalog and have them circle the types of things they like. Now you have some guidelines to go by.

Make and bake. No matter how your wallet flexes, consider giving handmade gifts or treats to extended family and friends. That personal touch is very appealing.

Plan for next Christmas now. Put away some money each month, depositing it into a holiday account at your bank or credit union. That'll take the pressure off for next December, and earn you some interest too.

Cheat Scrooge. Finish shopping and wrap presents before Thanksgiving, so you can enjoy the holidays. If parties are normally at your house, give yourself a year off; let someone else host.

Finish shopping before Thanksgiving, so you can enjoy the holidays.

How about a tip on preparing for special occasions throughout the rest of the year?

Erika, a daycare provider in northern California, shares this gem: "I keep my eyes peeled for holiday craft ideas for the entire year. I write the ones that I like down on my calendar, so I know exactly what day to make them with the kids. Then I use little sticky notes to write a list of craft supplies I'll need for each month, and stick the note on the specific month in my calendar. That way, when I turn the page for a new month, I already have my list of needed supplies and can gather them up at the beginning of each month."

By watching out for financial and time traps, you will sail through the holidays with both your emotional and bank accounts intact.

Homebodies Hint. Let's steal Erika's idea. Whether for holidays or someone's special birthday, have craft supplies available to place in tiny hands. The inexpensive gifts children create themselves are priceless. Take a few moments to brainstorm some craft projects you would like to make with your family over the coming year.

12

Garage Sale Etiquette

A humorous look at garage-saling

*S*ince *I adopted a stay-at-home mom's* tight budget several years ago, I've turned into a garage sale addict. At first I hesitated at the thought of purchasing other people's cast-offs. Then I started finding twenty-five-dollar jeans for twenty-five cents a pair, and I became a believer.

Wal-Mart looks expensive as I splash through piles of second-hand goodies. Sometimes I can barely see over the stack of nearly-new clothes as I head for my hostess's card table. Plopping them down, we sort through the miscellaneous items, peeling off stickers, jotting down prices and stuffing my bounty into a recycled department store bag. "Four dollars," she tallies as I smile.

I love it. Of course, as a wise woman once said, you have to kiss a lot of frogs to find a prince. That's especially true in garage-saling, as you sift through dirt to find diamonds. But just when you think you can't face one more driveway, you'll discover a box of gems. Right item, right size, right price. Sold! In an instant you're rejuvenated, scouring the ads for more sales.

I have noticed, however, that like everywhere else there are those who try to take all the fun out of this romp through neighbors' treasures. These boors need to read a few chapters on garage sale etiquette.

For instance, when the sign says the sale starts at eight a.m., that isn't code for "unless you pound on my door at six a.m." But there always seem to be garage sale guerrillas roaming the streets. Armed with maps, money and classified ads, they attack at dawn.

Engines idling, these people camp outside unsuspecting homes, ready to charge as soon as they detect any sign of life.

Meanwhile, inside, a sleepy hostess reaches for a cup of coffee. Up until two a.m. marking merchandise, she's recovering from yesterday's skirmishes with her kids, who suddenly bonded with stuff they haven't looked at in years. Yawning, she opens the blinds—then snaps them shut.

Ding dong.

If she's smart, she'll make them wait until she has had her breakfast. And read the paper. And watched a little bit of TV.

People bolt from their cars like horses at the racetrack.

Once the garage door goes up, people bolt from their cars like horses at the racetrack.

There are etiquette rules to keep in mind when you're the one having the garage sale too. Everyone but the most serious-minded folks understand that negotiating is half the fun. If you're in this to make money, it kills the spirit. *Please*: no ten-dollar toddler dresses! Customers are looking for diamonds in the dirt, not rubies in the showcase. Consider a consignment store to hawk the expensive stuff. Or make a visitor's day by pricing things so low that they'll be hugging you at the card table.

In case you're debating, yes, it is dishonest to put a tag over that hole in a shirt. Just mark it "as is." That way you don't have to feel guilty or worry about an angry confrontation later. Also, advertise truthfully. Don't say it is a "huge sale" if it isn't.

Now back to the buyers checking out the merchandise. Number one, it should not be done from the street, hanging out the driver's side window, taking inventory while rolling by. Running over a pedestrian definitely adds to the price tag.

Standing on tip-toe, peeking in garage windows the day before the sale is also prohibited.

Comments should be kept to a minimum. (Like Mom said, "If you can't say something nice . . .") Saying, "What a bunch of junk!" is always inappropriate (even if it's true).

If you discover it's not a bunch of junk and you land in the midst of garage sale heaven, refrain from trashing the tables and hogging everything. "Don't touch that . . . it's mine!" is not proper conversation between civilized shoppers.

"Don't touch that ... it's mine!" is not proper conversation.

If you need glasses, wear them. Holding up clearly tagged items and yelling, "How much is this?" irritates your hostess. Items marked "sold" are sold. And no, you can't go behind that curtain.

Leave the fifty-dollar bills at home. And unless you're a relative (sometimes, because you *are* a relative), your hostess shouldn't accept a check.

Other rules to remember: This is a garage sale, not a day-care—keep kids under control and off toys you are not planning to buy. Don't park on the grass or in the neighbor's driveway. Don't bring your dog. Thank your hostess, even if you don't buy anything.

And the most important rule of garage sale etiquette? No, you can't use their bathroom.

Now that we know the rules, go for it! Happy prospecting as you dig for those diamonds.

Homebodies Hint. Now is a good time to go through the closets and toy chests, sorting out things which are no longer used, but are still taking up space. Hold your own garage sale, then grab the kids and recycle your profits by hitting consignment shops, flea markets and neighborhood yard sales in search of the next great deal.

13

Money Under the Bed Liner

Updating instead of buying new

Terry and I saved fifteen thousand dollars the last time the I-wanna-new-car bug bit us. Here's how.

I've been home for quite a while now, almost a decade. Things aren't nearly as tight as they were that first year, thanks to regular raises at Terry's job and several years' practice in learning to live on one income.

As our budget began flexing a bit, Terry started letting the remote linger on new truck commercials. Fords, Chevys, GMCs; I could almost hear the horsepower galloping across our living room. At first I was nervous, but hey—he had been jockeying his 1985 Dodge Ram for years, and I figured with all the overtime he puts in, he was due for an upgrade. I joined Terry on the couch, watching the pretty pictures drive by.

We followed the TV ads onto a friendly lot, took a look at the new truck prices, resuscitated each other, then headed next door to the used trucks section.

Prospects weren't much better there: sixteen thousand dollars or more for a program (nearly new, lease-return) truck. But maybe with some creative financing and twenty years to pay, we could swing it.

As we continued talking ourselves into a possible purchase, Terry and I took a critical look at our trade-in. Hmm. Fifteen years can do a lot to a truck, no matter how well it runs.

Faded paint and rust patches, cracked upholstery and washed out interior door panels, bald tires, missing trim and peeling pinstripes. We had to face facts. The only way we would get anything out of this nag would be if we parked it close to the new truck lot and snagged someone blindly stumbling around with sticker shock.

It's time to spend money to make money.

It was time to spend money to make money. Scheduling an appointment with a local discount paint shop, we had them buff out the rust and give the Dodge a new coat of charcoal gray, along with fresh pinstripes. The interior door panels were re-dyed, then accented with a colorful slipcover and mats. Old or missing trim was replaced with shiny edging. By the time we added deep-treaded new tires, we were in love.

Forget about giving up this truck. Instead of a clunker, Terry was now driving a classic. And instead of paying sixteen thousand dollars or more for a program truck, we had spent a little under a thousand to spruce up the reliable one we already owned.

It was fun too. In my quest to be a frugal-minded mom, I am always trying to look beyond the obvious. Imagination is a real asset to parents who are trying to stay home with their kids.

For example, Gretchen, an Air Force wife and at-home mom, had her eye on a jogging stroller, but was discouraged by the two-hundred-dollar price tag.

"I do a lot of walking and rollerblading, so I really wanted one," Gretchen says. "I searched and searched for the right one with the right price at a garage sale, but wasn't having any luck. My husband found one that someone had put out on their curb for the trash man. It was a bit rusted, two tires were flat and the material needed washing.

"I quickly took all the material off and washed it while my husband ran out and purchased some inexpensive sandpaper, spray paint and a couple of tire tubes. The tires were in excellent shape. So we then scrubbed it clean, sanded the rust out, spray painted it, fixed the tires, and it looks brand new!

Is there a classic hiding under some old paint?

"I took it for a spin today for the first time, and it is like an SUV of strollers," Gretchen laughs. "We went off-roading and everything!"

Think about your own car, home and furniture. Do you really need new? Or is there a classic hiding under some old paint? If you are concerned about getting the most bang for your buck, see what it will take to fix up what you've already got before you reach for the credit cards or loan applications. Maybe like me, you'll save fifteen thousand dollars this month.

Homebodies Hint. Go through your house and imagine what the place would look like if you rearranged or refurbished some items. Be creative, moving some items to different rooms and rescuing others from their banished-to-the-attic state. If you need to spend some money, go with relatively inexpensive choices (paint, stain, border, etc.) to update your surroundings.

14

Single
Stay-at-Home
Parents

Exploring your options

*I*t *goes without saying* that if you want to stay home with your kids, you need to have a working spouse.

Or do you?

Once again we run into one of those situations where conventional wisdom can keep us from even looking at our options. Yes, it is more difficult to be an at-home parent when you're single, but it is not impossible. Some single mothers work from home; others start in-home daycares; still others turn to government and church-based assistance that enables them to take care of their young children until they start school.

"There's nothing in Scripture that may lead us to believe that after divorce, there is something wrong in desiring to be

It's more difficult, but not impossible, to be a single at-home parent.

home with our children," says Sandra, who is raising three children (ages eight, fourteen and sixteen) on her own in North Carolina. "When we are obedient to that calling, the Lord will show us what to do."

Blending child support payments, frugal living and cleaning houses two days a week while her children are in school, Sandra has been able to maximize her time with them. She follows a precise budget, and only works the amount she needs to pay the bills. "I could clean houses five or six days a week, but that would defeat my purpose for being home."

Money poses a constant challenge, but she meets it head on. "I'm not going to sit here and think that because I'm being obedient to my calling and staying home with my kids, money is just going to flow into the mailbox," Sandra says. "There's responsibility—keeping the thermostat turned down, budgeting, doing all the coupon stuff, taking clothes to the consignment store. Maybe one night a week, we'll have pizza. But that'll be the night a large is on sale for $6.99."

Sandra's teens understand the financial situation and do their best to help out. "My sixteen-year-old got a job to help provide for his car insurance and gas money. He also buys most of his own stuff," she notes. Sometimes Sandra is floored by the generosity her children show each other. "At Christmas each of my boys came to me separately, saying, 'Mom, don't buy a present for me. Use the money for the other two.'"

Chores pose an interesting challenge when there's only one parent present. When Sandra encounters something she can't do, like replacing a damaged door, she asks for help. She acknowledges the hesitancy to appear needy. "But as single mothers, we have to allow people to enter into this journey with us," Sandra says. She turned to her small group at church. "If I had not been able to share where I was at, they would never have known where to offer to help."

It is also important to Sandra to help others. She couldn't afford to pay the friends who fixed her door, but she was able to bake fresh pies and write a letter about "earthly angels" to thank them. She may clean a house as a shower gift for a new mom or prepare a meal for a family that's under the weather. "Single moms without a lot of money may think they can't participate in their church's ministry. But sometimes we disengage from things in life that will reward us back."

Emotional support is critical. "There aren't a lot of pats on the back for stay-at-home moms, normally. Many single stay-at-home mothers have a lot of trouble with this, because their self-esteem is hurt by divorce."

> Look for God in the circumstance you're in.

A woman's standard of living often drops dramatically after a death or divorce. "Usually you have to move from your home, where your security has been," Sandra says. And loneliness will set in, even when mom gets to spend lots of time with her children. "As a single stay-at-home mother, you especially need that adult time. Get with other women; go to a friend's home, see an early matinee or share meals. Or just go window-shopping together.

"Don't make this a solo journey," Sandra counsels. "I have a choice as to whether I will allow myself to become overwhelmed by this situation. Instead of always looking to find myself in another set of circumstances, I look for God in the circumstance I'm in. I can't, but he can!

"We can't do this by ourselves. We need our relationship

with the Lord, we need our relationship with our friends, and we need our relationship with our kids."

As Sandra recently helped her fourteen-year-old son, Ryan, print out an English paper on his feelings and goals, her heart jumped when she read what he had written. "I don't know what the future holds, but what I know is that God has a plan for me," Ryan wrote. "I know life will have its twists and turns, but if I follow God it will be okay, because I've seen that in my own family."

Such is the hope and promise of all single stay-at-home mothers who take Christ up on his offer to be a husband to the husbandless and a father to the fatherless. "Our family doesn't look like what it used to, and that hurts," Sandra says. "But when I look at my children and God, I still see family."

Homebodies Hint. Don't assume that as a single parent there's no way you can stay home with your children. Do the math, look at work-at-home options, and surround yourself with supportive people who can help you reach your goals.

PART 3

Examining Your
Work Options

*"The top motivation
spurring parents into home businesses
is the dream of spending more time
with their families
while maintaining skills and contacts
within their field.
Establishing guidelines is essential,
though, because it is so easy
to get over-amped."*

15

Scheduling
Quality Time

*Focusing on family
instead of career*

*S*ometimes—*usually after an especially* tough
day around the house with the kids—some at-home parents
start idealizing their past work experience. As they remember
it, their bosses were accommodating, their careers rewarding,
their finances fit. Sounds a lot more attractive than a screaming baby, an unfinished to-do list and a tight wallet, doesn't it?

But the reality is, no matter where you work—whether in
or outside the home—there are good days and bad days. Personally, I decided a long time ago that overall, being at home is
better for me. Reflecting on my working-mom days sparks the
impulse to grab Terry and make him promise he'll never make
me go back!

If you'd told me in college that I'd ever feel like this, I would have laughed in your face. I used to love office life. But that was before I was dropping my screaming toddler off at daycare every morning and avoiding one-last-change bosses at night. When I did finally arrive home after dodging freeway maniacs, grabbing groceries and praying I would make it to daycare before it closed, I had little left to give my likewise over-stimulated kids.

I was having trouble finding that elusive balance between work and family.

There are lots of women who do it every day, but I was having trouble finding that elusive balance between work and family.

Painfully aware that my boss was getting the lion's share of my attention, I constantly searched for ways to squeeze more kid time into my schedule.

For instance, when Carrie was a nursing infant, I hired a sitter a few minutes away from my office. Straight up noon, I left papers fluttering on my desk as I zoomed out to the employee parking lot. At 12:07 I was running up the sitter's stairs. Moments later Carrie was in my arms and I could relax for forty-six minutes. Then, ready or not, I was out the door again, my baby howling in the background as I leapt into my car and sped back to the office.

Once Carrie outgrew breastfeeding, I transferred her to the same daycare where her big sister, Karen, stayed before and after school. My lunch hour became more diversified. I could either zip over to the daycare center (ten minutes away) to play a quick game of peek-a-boo with Carrie, pop in at Karen's school (hit the lights right, fourteen minutes) to share a sandwich, or race to our house (a twelve-minute sprint), throw in a load of laundry, dust like a madwoman and start the crock pot.

Weekdays were crammed with projects, chores and relationships. Each night I pulled the covers over my head and collapsed into a fitful six hours of sleep. Saturdays were catch-up days; Sundays boiled over with church obligations.

What a life! Maxed out. Stressed out. Worn out. I was out and out ready for a change. Becoming a stay-at-home mom started looking extremely attractive.

Believe me, I worked hard to get my degree, and in the beginning I enjoyed the stimulation of a fast-paced workplace. But the births of my children ushered in a new era, one in which I was torn apart as I tried to give 100 percent to both my boss and my family.

> **Maxed out.
> Stressed out.
> Worn out.
> I was out and
> out ready for
> a change.**

It can't be done. At least, I wasn't able to reconcile the necessary division of a normal day, say six a.m. to nine p.m.:

6-7 a.m. Get everyone up, fed and ready to go; drop kids at daycare.

7 a.m.-6 p.m. Drive to work, put in a full day (including the daily lunchtime marathon), pick up the kids, drive home.

6-7 p.m. Make dinner, check homework, eat, clean up kitchen.

7-8 p.m. Family time.

8-9 p.m. Baths, books and bed. Lights out.

That makes twelve hours linked to work and three hours partially dedicated to my kids.

What's wrong with this picture?

I guess it's all right, as long as those three hours are quality time. But if a full day's work, followed by a jaunt to the convenience store and plowing through a dozen loads of laundry hadn't already done me in, I didn't have much left to give Karen and Carrie. They were also tired after their own long stretch away from home.

Since I have become an at-home mom, I am available to my

girls all day. Granted, "all day" is sometimes twenty-three hours longer than I feel up to. But those over-amped periods are rare. Usually I'm thrilled to be present for the elusive quality hours that can't be scheduled, which arrive on their own timetable.

"For everything there is a season, and a time for every purpose under heaven" (Ecclesiastes 3:1). Right now it is my parenting season. I suspect I'll someday plunge back into a career outside the home. In the meantime, however, I'm happy to simply invest in my little ones here on the home front.

Homebodies Hint. Lasso true quality time with each of your children during this coming week. Whether it's going on a picnic, reading a book together, talking heart to heart or enjoying some other bonding activity, remember to hold your child close and assure them of their priority in your life.

16

Delaying
Your Departure

Resisting
working-mother guilt

I think everybody has experienced the sensation at one time or another. It's that "what's wrong with this picture?" feeling that seeps over us when we are mismatched to our situation. Maybe you are a country person transplanted to the city, a gregarious fun-lover tiptoeing around a monastery or a homebody stuck in downtown traffic, heading to the office.

Whatever the dynamics, the unshakeable impression is, "I don't belong here."

"In the environment that I work in (corporate dog-eat-dog-don't-turn-your-back-on-anyone-if-you-know-what's-good-for-you world), I stick out like a three-headed Martian," says Kathleen, who works in a high-powered Pennsylvania publishing office. "When I mention my goal is to be home with my girls, people actually laugh."

Kathleen is undeterred, however, and continues to contemplate an alternative at-home lifestyle. The challenge for Kathleen and any other parent presently delayed in their quest to come home is to keep focused on the goal, remaining open to possibilities as they present themselves.

"I almost became obsessed with the desire to be a full-time mommy."

A positive attitude is critical. Listen to this anonymous mom who felt herself slipping into despair because she couldn't quit work right away: "I thought about it constantly. Prayed about it all the time. Sought advice on how to do it. I almost became obsessed with the desire to be a full-time mommy. I found myself throwing away the happiness that God was giving me daily. As a matter of fact, I was throwing it away with both hands. I didn't enjoy my children, my husband, my students, my friends or my church. I didn't have time to enjoy those things. I had to find a way to come home!"

Likewise, guilt—that pervasive snake—likes to slither up the backs of unhappy working moms. After Christmas break Kathleen's six-year-old started having stomachaches. "Many of the kids were acting out in this way after spending lots of time over the holidays with their usually working parents," she said. "Elizabeth just wanted me home. And I did too. I felt horrible, not being able to pick her up!" Then her daughter admitted she wasn't really sick. "I told her I wasn't mad at her, but it wasn't right to fib, even if she wanted to be with me and not at the after-school program. I thought we had gotten over that hurdle! I felt guilty, like I was such a bad mom."

Having been a working mom myself for six years, I can empathize with Kathleen's worries. But I think we should cut ourselves some slack. Sure, becoming a full-time, at-home mom is a worthy and admirable goal. But for many women who want to attain that status, it will take time. There are plans to be laid; bills to be paid. Rare is the woman who decides today that she wants to be home and tomorrow finds herself there.

Don't let stress spur you into a rash decision. Quitting a job without first planning for the transition is tantamount to committing financial suicide, and it helps no one, least of all your children. So what do you do in the meantime? You do the very best you can with the situation you're in. If circumstances won't allow you to quit work all at once, aim at putting in fewer hours.

Kathleen has been giving it some thought. "As I was outside at 6 a.m., scraping my car off and shaking the snow out of my boots, I was thinking how much I wished I was inside with the girls all warm and snuggly. Instead, I'm outside in my PJ's

> Don't let stress spur you into a rash decision.

hoping the weather conditions don't make me late for work and I don't miss my meeting. I kept thinking (as I tend to do when I am on the verge of frostbite) how very much I want to at least work at home, if even part time."

Keep looking at that schedule. Where can you cut? Can you work four days instead of five? Thirty hours instead of forty? A straight forty-hour week, instead of regularly sticking around for overtime?

Yes, it would be great to have the flexibility available to a full-time, at-home parent. But don't discount the benefits of small steps in that direction. Imagine a child's reaction if his mother was able to shave even five hours a week off her work schedule, then spend that entire five hours with him. Most youngsters would be bouncing on the beds in delight!

As you are working toward your dream of coming home, here are some tips on carving precious minutes out of your full-time working schedule:

☐ Reduce drive time by taking a job closer to home.

☐ Take a half-hour lunch, and get off earlier or come in later.

☐ Negotiate with your employer to see if you can do some or all of your work from home.

☐ Develop your own home-based business.

Your focus is on what's important. Periodically review your options, do the best you can with today's realities, and never give up your dream to eventually become an at-home parent.

Homebodies Hint. Sit down with your spouse and examine your work schedules. What are some things you can do to increase family time now as you continue to move toward the ultimate goal of having one parent home?

17

Mothering Other Women's Children

Becoming an in-home daycare provider

It's 5:50 p.m., and several cars are in the driveway as Linda pulls up in front of her sitter's house. Exhausted from fighting bumper-to-bumper traffic after another stressful day at work, she turns off the ignition and sits still for a moment.

Laughter drifts in her open window, carried from the backyard where some children are swinging while others roll across the lawn. She sees the sitter supervising the play, while greeting another parent who has come to pick up her son. Suddenly inspiration strikes. "I could do that!" Linda's mind starts racing as she considers starting her own in-home daycare. "I'd be able to stay home all day with my kids and watch a couple of others to bring in some extra money."

Linda's impulse is not unusual. Many stay-at-home wanna-bes get the same idea. But is it the right move for you? And more important, is it the right move for the "couple of others" you'll be helping raise?

"Running a daycare is terrific in the aspect that you are home meeting your own children's needs, and have no travel or clothing expenses, other than a normal wardrobe," says Merrie, who was an in-home daycare provider for several years. "It is rewarding for a nurturing person who loves children. The downfalls are lack of privacy, wear and tear on your house and belongings, isolation, and—typical of being self-employed—having no one to fill in for you if you are ill.

"Expenses include licensing and extra insurance for your vehicle and home, cleaning supplies, toys and equipment, food, field trips and entertainment, and safety proofing for your home and yard (such as fencing and locks). Daycare is a good source of income, if you can handle it. It is not for the easily stressed, or for a low threshold of tolerance or low energy person."

Merrie recommends linking up with other people who are doing the same thing. "There are many communities with support groups for home daycare providers. Some also serve as referral services, which decreases the need for advertising."

Make sure you have the correct temperament and motives.

If you do decide to open a daycare, make sure you have the correct temperament and motives. "Before I was blessed with the opportunity to be home with my little ones, my children had been in every childcare situation imaginable: nannies to in-home daycare to large corporate preschools to state-funded after school programs," remembers Kass.

"During that time I developed a wonderful relationship with a lady named Sherrie. She took care of my boys, Matthew and David, for three years. She was a single mom who built her daycare business so she could work at home, pay the mortgage and be there for her teenager.

> Be someone's Godsend in their childcare/full-time-working-mom turmoil.

"Sherrie was a Godsend in my childcare/full-time-working-mom turmoil. She dealt with my boys at their best and their worst. Because of her compassion, dedication and resourcefulness, we became very close.

"My boys and I continue to visit her now that I'm home. She has been very supportive in helping me plan my own in-home daycare. When she found out I was homeschooling, she started sending me extra craft projects for the boys, educational materials and other resources. What a gem! We trade coupons, keep each other updated on free stuff to do with the kids, and we're hoping to go on field trips together.

"If I hadn't worked outside the home and had to search high and low for a good childcare provider, I would never have had such a wonderful friend," Kass says. "And I never would have thought of returning to the childcare field to be there for other moms."

"Overall, I feel very appreciative of my daycare moms and kids," says Suzanne, who watches two boys who are just a few months older than her little girl. "If they did not trust me with the care of their children, I could not afford to stay home with my daughter. Plus, it feels really great to play such an important role in the lives of these other children."

As Kass and Sherrie discovered, mothers' lives can be enhanced when the daycare provider reaches out to the parent as well as the child. Dana started her in-home daycare when she left the medical field about five years ago. "I have been encouraged by the moms as much as I have ministered to them," she says, "because they keep me searching and delving into things, trying to become better at what I do.

"We don't just have a worker/employer-type arrangement or service exchange," Dana notes. "I'm the stand-in mom." She has a quiet period during the early afternoon while the kids are down for naps and uses e-mail to let parents know what's been going on that day. "It comforts them to have that contact."

There isn't a revolving door at pick-up time either. Dana knows that pent-up anger over work issues can spill over into family time, so she asks parents how their day went. "I see their struggles as working mothers. Sometimes they need to vent, so they sit down and talk to me. If their spouse is out of town, they may even stay for dinner."

As you can see from these examples, becoming an excellent in-home daycare provider entails much more than changing diapers and reading books. Remember that watching other mothers' kids all day can be stressful and will definitely limit the amount of one-on-one time you have with your own children. But it can also be an extremely rewarding experience for those who have a gift in this area, and a true blessing to the people they touch.

Homebodies Hint. If you're thinking about becoming an in-home daycare provider, take a close look at your gifts and motivations before you take the plunge. Is this the best choice for you—and for the families you'll be meeting?

18

Part-Time Practicalities

A realistic look at working part time

If you've done all you can to cut your bills and still don't have enough money to cover your necessary expenses, it's time to consider a part-time job. Don't feel guilty! You're not abandoning your kids; you're providing for them. As your financial situation improves, you can continue to scale back your hours—cut, cut, cut—until you're home full time again.

As you start looking, be aware that there are schemers who prey on moms who want to work at home. (Read chapter nineteen for more on this topic.) And once you find that ideal part-time opportunity, remember that nothing's perfect. Just like working full time or staying home full time, there are pluses and minuses, good days and bad days. Understanding and accepting the challenges of working part time will increase

Part time
is better
than
bankruptcy.

your chances of enjoying the experience.

Match your strengths to the job. Do this even if you're only working a few hours a week. Since I have a strong administrative/computer background, I use those skills whenever I need to work part time. For instance, I've done overflow typing, taught computer classes and written freelance articles. I also did before- and after-school childcare. But I didn't enjoy it. That's because I don't have a gift for entertaining little kids. Likewise, I hate making (and being the subject of) product pitches. So I'm not likely to be successful as a Tupperware or Amway demonstrator.

Expect reduced—or no—employee benefits. Jeanette's company gave her the option of reducing her hours from forty to twenty. "My husband feels pretty good about my staying more at home; he's prayed God would enable this for some time," Jeanette says. "The major challenge is that although I'll receive half vacation, half sick days and so on, I'll lose all health and pension benefits. To compensate, my boss is coming up a little bit in salary."

As Jeanette points out, employers are often reluctant to provide full coverage for part-time employees. The good news is, if you're going the opposite direction (from an at-home parent to a part-timer), you may go from no benefits to at least partial coverage.

Plan to work at your work-at-home job. "A lot of women get starry-eyed about how a stay-at-home job gives them flexibility," says Amy, who makes and sells candles. "They can do what they want and work when they want. That's true, but it's still work and just like any other job, you will get paid according to the amount you do." Amy remembers several situations where friends' work-at-home projects fizzled because they didn't discipline themselves, failing to spend the time and effort necessary to build the business.

Avoid the pitfalls of opposite shifts. You might be considering working a part-time evening job, thinking that you'll watch the kids during the day while your husband works, then he can watch them while you're gone. On the surface this sounds like a great arrangement—the children are never in daycare.

Expect to work at your work-at-home job.

But be careful. Absence does not make the heart grow fonder. Absence makes the heart grow resentful. Sometimes we get in trouble by focusing too much on the kids and not enough on mom and dad. Whatever schedule you and your spouse are on, build in quality and quantity time for the two of you, alone. A peck on the cheek as the baby is passed from one parent to the other isn't going to cut it.

Remember, kids take more time than you think. "If you've got preschoolers, don't try to work part-time from home unless you have access to at least some childcare," advises Teresa, a Kansas work-at-home mother with two boys, Zephan (two) and Kaden (four months). "Otherwise, you'll be working double-time! You'll go insane, unless you've got a small job that can be done during their naps."

As Teresa mentioned, our projects can take twice as long if we're trying to watch our children at the same time we're working on something that demands our complete attention. "I'd much rather have my boys go to a neighbor's house for a few hours, allowing me dedicated work time, so that I can focus entirely on them when we're together," she says.

Julie, whose children are now nine and eleven, gave piano

lessons when her kids were toddlers. "One of my twelve-year-old students would come over and play with the kids during lessons (in my home, so I was still there if they really needed something). My kids never thought she was coming to baby-sit; they just thought she was coming to play. It worked like a charm, and I was able to teach Monday through Friday, from four to six o'clock this way."

Suzanne enlists her husband's help. "One evening a week, I go upstairs and work on my marketing job while he plays with our daughter. I can hear them downstairs laughing, so I know it has been good for their relationship.

"Another thing moms might try is to establish a routine every day where they work at the computer for an hour or so while their child watches a favorite program, colors nearby or does something else to entertain her," Suzanne suggests. "If you're really consistent with the routine, the child will probably learn to play by herself for that time so mom can work."

Be realistic about what you can accomplish. Not every profession is geared for part-time employees. So reroute your skills into family-friendly ventures that are related to the areas in which you excel. Also remember that an eighteen-month-old requires much more hands-on attention than a four-year-old. The time you have available to invest in a part-time job will expand as your children grow.

Homebodies Hint. If you decide to pursue a part-time job, be realistic about the pros and cons involved. Then choose a job that will mesh well with your particular situation and skills.

19

Skip the Scams

Finding legitimate work-at-home opportunities

*A*s *a California mom still searching* for that perfect work-at-home opportunity, Bernie isn't jaded yet, but she's close. "The last three companies I contacted all claimed to have fabulous products that everyone needed," she says. "There were no sales pitches involved. All I had to do was tell other people about these wonderful products and my money would roll in. The problem was, I also had to purchase a minimum of $50 of these products in order to benefit from others selling them. The company was getting their money whether I made any or not.

"Then I received a brochure in the mail about a wonderful opportunity to learn a secret way of reducing my (and others') grocery bills. All I had to do was send in $65.95 for the secret manual. And this was a 50% discount off the regular price!" Bernie laughs.

"Am I sounding sarcastic? I hope so; many of these companies take your $65.95 or whatever for mysterious money-making packages and then you don't hear from them again.

"I'm certain there are legitimate work-at-home opportunities out there; we just need to keep looking. However, please be wary of the quick-money, just-send-in-a-check, get-rich-easy offers you read and hear about. The companies get rich quickly, not you."

It takes a scummy person to exploit a cash-strapped stay-at-home mom. But believe me, there are a lot of predators out there. So keep your guard up; don't let anyone steal your money or your hope.

Start your search by contacting companies and people you know personally. One of the best places to find a legitimate work-at-home job is through a former employer. Look beyond the department you used to work in. Some other areas in the company may have more flexibility in scheduling work-at-home projects. Nothing available? Put together your own detailed plan, carefully noting duties, costs and advantages to both the company and yourself. Then present it to your old boss and the staff in human resources.

Contact companies and people you know personally.

If they're not receptive to using you as a telecommuting employee, pitch yourself as a self-employed consultant doing the same job. Consultants are usually better paid than employees, too, since the company doesn't have to provide benefits or workspace.

You might also touch base with coworkers who are no longer with the company. "Until I started teaching preschool two mornings a week at my son's school, I did overflow typing for a newly-formed company and made twelve dollars an hour," says Carol, who works part time in Mississippi. "They were very reputable; I knew two of them from a previous job. I had to pay my own taxes and Social Security from the twelve dollars, but I could also write off certain expenses such as mileage. So I averaged bringing home about ten dollars an hour.

"It was great because I didn't have to leave home, other than to run by their office once a week. I didn't have to have childcare, and I could work the hours I wanted to. I did this for almost three years, until the company was large enough to hire more full-time employees. As a plus, they are constantly calling me now and have offered me a full- or part-time position in their office."

"I truly believe the opportunities are out there, though sometimes you have to create them for yourself," says Suzanne, who does marketing from home (sending out mailings, making phone calls, etc.) for an area businesswoman. "I found this job opportunity by chance, since she is my neighbor. But if you know of any businesses where they need help to find clients, you might be able to get something like this started.

Create opportunities for yourself.

"The other job I used to do was news monitoring. I got paid nine to twelve dollars per hour to summarize local news shows, which I taped. It's a very easy job if you're a fast typist and are observant. If you live in a major metropolitan area, I'll bet there is a news monitoring service near you. Lots of times they don't advertise those types of jobs because they get bombarded, since everyone and their dog wants to work at home."

"Do you have a talent that you can tap to provide a service in your community?" Julie asks. "Art, decorating, sewing, childcare, music, gardening, landscaping? I have found that service-oriented businesses are easier to start than product-based sales."

Work-at-Home Moms.com president Cheryl Demas advises: "The number one thing to remember is 'Don't send money.' You should never have to pay someone to work for them. I don't care what they call it—money for software, money to prove you are serious, a processing fee—whatever. Just don't do it.

"Of course, there are legitimate direct sales organizations who do charge a fee for your starter kit, but they should be very specific about exactly what you will receive and how you will make money. They should also have a clear return policy."

The Council of Better Business Bureaus also warns consumers to

> beware of falling prey to tempting work-at-home promotions that offer "easy money." You could be at risk for some very bad consequences. You can:
>
> **Lose money.** Consumers have lost amounts ranging from $10 to $70,000, or more.
>
> **Waste valuable time.** You may throw away countless hours on worthless projects that cost you a lot of money to attempt and complete, but, in the end, give you nothing in return.
>
> **Ruin your reputation.** You might be selling your customers terrible quality merchandise or nonexistent services.
>
> **Be a target of legal action.** You can be held liable for perpetrating a fraud by deliberately or even unintentionally promoting and selling fraudulent products or services to others. (Council of Better Business Bureau, *Work-at-Home Schemes,* 2000)

Remember, just like in baseball, you shouldn't swing at every pitch. Let the scams slide by. Wait for the right setup, then score with your at-home business.

Homebodies Hint. It may take a while to find a profitable work-at-home job, but as technology continues to improve, opportunities will expand.

20

Attack of the Killer Home Business

Balancing demands of an in-home business

*W*orking at home sounds attractive to a lot of people, and it can be a great choice for family-focused parents. But there are pitfalls too. As you are pursuing that perfect blend of work and kids, beware of the dreaded attack of the killer home business!

The top motivation spurring parents into home businesses is the dream of spending more time with their families while maintaining skills and contacts within their field. Establishing guidelines is essential, though, because it is so easy to get over-amped. It's not unusual to have this vision of keeping our foot in the door at work, then realize we've given our entire being over to stomping out our future career niche instead.

Let me plug myself into this example. It is my heart's desire to raise my children as an at-home parent. However, I also love writing, and I'm sure any future career beyond raising my kids will involve the publishing business. My constant battle, and I think the battle of anyone who has a home-based business, is to remember that family comes first.

If I get angry because my child wants me to play Barbies with her, but I would rather finish up my article on how precious

My constant battle is to remember that family comes first.

it is when stay-at-home mothers spend quality time with their kids, then I've got a serious problem.

Persistent anxiety is another signal that we've bitten off more work-at-home business than we can handle. Look at these anonymous comments left on the Homebodies message boards:

> I always have people telling me they wish they could work from home. When they say it, they make it sound so *perfect*. But they don't realize how hard this is. If you leave your child at daycare, you get to concentrate more on work. But here, my house yells at me. Also, I try to keep up with the kids from my office, so I'm not able to concentrate as well. I've been doing this for four years now, and it's tough.

If I were to write a response, it would read as follows:

> Your house is "yelling," your kids are distracting you, and you can't concentrate on work *because your priorities are out of whack.* (Don't feel singled out; like I already said, I've been there too.) Instead of concentrating on family, home and business, you're chasing business, home and family. It's the same habit many of us had when we were working outside the home.

Patti experienced more of a sneak-attack from her home-based freelancing business. When her children were very young, she spent lots of time with them and very little time on her writing. As the children grew, so did her perceived discretionary time for work projects. "I no longer had a toddler to pull at my pant leg or to climb up into my lap while I was working. And my family was really good about it. So it was easy to go back to the computer after supper and work well into the night.

"But as I was typing away one day, I had a sudden realization," Patti remembers. "My family was moving around all about me, and I was not a part of the group setting. They were talking to each other and asking each other for help. Sometimes they'd throw in a word or two to me and hear me answer, 'Just a minute, I'm busy right now . . .'

Don't lose sight of the real reasons you're home.

"It hit me then. Busy? Too busy for them? Why, my whole reason for working at home was to be there for my family! Now that I had this sudden insight, I needed to regroup."

Patti took a day off to do some revamping. "I took a good long look at the way our family life had changed since I began working from home. I found that my projects were consuming my life. I recognized that I had to set some boundaries so I didn't lose sight of my real reasons for working at home.

"I wrote down all my different responsibilities that I need to get done during a given day, including business obligations and deadlines, household duties and a little free time for myself when everyone is gone. I switched and swapped and juggled all over the place until I came up with a tentative schedule for a normal week."

Now Patti uses that schedule to help keep her priorities straight. "Every morning I look at the schedule and see what is slotted for the day. I do the time-sensitive and important duties first, leaving the odds and ends until later in the day. I try to be done with all my projects by the time school is out."

A home business run amuck sours relationships with the people we love most. But when pursued properly, the same business can add flavor to family life by providing more spending money, developing communication skills and opening possible ministry opportunities.

Homebodies Hint. As you develop or overhaul your work priorities, define the boundaries that keep a potentially killer home business contained.

PART 4

Raising Your Children

*"I will be eternally grateful
that we've managed to raise
children we love,
but also children that we
like and respect.
It has made all of the
hard work worth it."*

21

The Long Arm
of the Maw

Setting moral boundaries

*B*efore I had kids, I used to gasp at those harnesses some mothers attach to their wandering children. You know, the ones that look like little doggie leashes.

I kept expecting a harnessed toddler to flop on his back and struggle out of his restraint like a double-jointed cat, whipping this way and that until he was free. But usually both mother and child would pass by, one confidently holding the loop while the other explored the outer boundary of his tethered world.

"Child abuse," I would whisper to another knowing and likewise childless friend. We frowned as the odd couple went on their way.

Since the birth of my own rambunctious offspring, I've lost my superior attitude.

You haven't really experienced parenthood until you've chased your two-year-old down the aisle at the local supermarket. Wishing I had arms like an octopus, I learned to salvage tossed oranges and replace tumbled cereal boxes while pursuing my pint-sized escapee. After planting my runaway securely in the grocery cart, I would roll a few feet, step away for just a second, then return to a basketful of squished bread and oozing, teeth-marked bananas.

And I had prayed for this baby.

Leashes at the mall began to make sense as I caught my daredevil daughter scaling the upper tier railing at the local shopping center. From within the circular clothes rack at department stores, she grinned as I frantically searched for her. "Peek-a-boo, Mommy!"

No knick knack had a life expectancy over five minutes when my toddler was in the room. Nervous hostesses eyed us as I steered my baby away from breakables, with more sturdy items strung in her wobbly wake.

With another year came more opportunities to reach out and touch my child—before she careened her Big Wheel out into the street, for instance. Or when she realized it was easier to climb up the phone books and pillows piled on a chair than it was to maneuver back down once she was finished rifling the kitchen cabinets.

I'm not sure when moms are supposed to reel in their tentacles. My toddler has grown to a preteen. Thankfully she no longer knocks boxes off store shelves, although she still grabs sweets and stows them in the cart. My emphasis now is navigating her away from negative attitudes and opinions, while piloting her toward that which is good in life. I wish there was a leash I could use to keep her within those boundaries! (She has a mom who loves her, though, and so far, she has responded well to my gentle harness.)

Trish, whose two boys are eight and ten, sees bedtime, riding in the car and sitting at the table as ideal settings for tender tugs on the reins. "We use these times to talk and build relationships with each other," she says. "My husband and I feel it is important to not only make our beliefs, values and rules plain, but to also let the kids know why we believe the way we do, have the values we have and set the rules we set. In the future, when we are not by their side, we hope they will then know why they must make the right choices."

Trish and her husband understand how important it is to let their children fail, acknowledge mistakes and then try again. "The choices they are allowed to make change as they grow older. We discuss their options and the consequences of their choices, then allow them to make the final decision. For example, our oldest son recently had the opportunity to take wrestling for several weeks. It is his favorite sport. He was already enrolled in choir two nights a week, participated in a Wednesday night kids club, and volunteered at church on Sunday. We allowed him to make the decision. He decided not to wrestle this year because he did not want his grades to slip due to spending too much of his energy on other activities. Hooray!"

Make your beliefs, values and rules plain.

Though she was proud of him for making the right choice, Trish knows there will be times when her sons will disappoint both their parents and themselves. "Sometimes their decisions are not the right ones, and they have to suffer the consequences. The rest of us might have to suffer a little too. But it is easier for them to learn from their mistakes now than it will be in the future, when the stakes could be much higher."

Gaye's children are grown, and she observes the preschoolers around her through loving but realistic eyes. "One thing I would encourage parents of very young children to keep in mind regarding discipline is to look at their behavior and ask yourself, 'Will this be cute at twelve or sixteen?' If the answer is no, then it should not be cute at two.

Will this be cute at twelve or sixteen? If not, then it should not be cute at two.

"At tender ages most behavioral problems can be managed with consistency, firmness and appropriate discipline," she points out. By the time they're teenagers, "let's just say one's odds of doing so drop horrifically and the methods required make the terrible twos look like a cake walk."

It can be tough to be the unpopular disciplinarian, but consistently applying guidance, fairness and love does pay off. "I feel humbled by the joy I have found in my children," Gaye says. "I will be eternally grateful that we've managed to raise children we love, but also children that we like and respect. It has made all of the hard work worth it."

Homebodies Hint. Think of a specific recent incidence where you were able to steer your child away, either physically or mentally, from something that could potentially harm them. What were the long-term benefits of your stepping in?

22

Not in My House, You Don't

Resisting ungodly societal trends

*E*very week or so I take a deep breath and dive into my seventh-grader's eighty-pound backpack. It's a jungle in there; rarely does anything enter and come out again unscathed. But I am determined to stay on top of her school work, so I take my chances with finger-snapping textbooks, sweaty gym clothes and half-eaten sandwiches. It's a dirty job, but mom's gotta do it.

On one such excursion I was hacking my way through a tangle of crumpled test papers when I noticed a thick novel crammed into one of her dozen three-ring binders.

"What's that?" I asked conversationally.

"I don't know," she answered.

Now my daughter is a preteen, which means she knows absolutely everything. My radar went up. Tugging the suspicious novel out of the binder, I turned it over and my heart sank. It was one of those popular witchcraft horror-based books that are expressly forbidden in the Gochnauer household.

I didn't know whether to yell or cry. My daughter didn't know whether to look at the ceiling or the floor; she just knew she didn't want to look at *me*.

It's a dirty job, but mom's gotta do it.

I decided not to yell or cry. Instead, I held the out-of-bounds book and got very quiet inside. Here we go again. It was another one of those teachable moments. My daughter and I had talked about this subject before, as I counseled her about how important it is to be selective about the activities we watch, read about and participate in. But it had been a while. In fact, as I thought about it, it had probably been over a year since we had covered this specific subject.

Not a long time to a forty-year-old mom, but an eternity to an absorb-the-world, hormone-charged preteen.

I set the novel on the table. "I'll return this to the school library for you," I said, removing the temptation. "When you get home tonight, we'll talk. I don't want to just say 'no' without you understanding why I feel this should be off limits. And I want to get inside your mind a little bit, so you can share with me what it is that makes this kind of book seem attractive to you."

My daughter nodded, then headed out to the bus stop, her overloaded backpack a smidgen lighter. She had a lot to think about before our conversation that night.

Censorship? Absolutely. If there is any place in this world where we should applaud censorship, it is in the parenting arena. No matter what we do or where we go, regardless of position or authority, we will never have a better opportunity to shape another human being.

It is a tough subject, though. Take a dozen sets of parents, and

you will have twelve different opinions on
what is okay and what isn't. How to act,
what to wear; who to hang with, where to go.
So many choices, so little consistent direction. Some of my best friends have no problem at all with the same series of books that
make my skin crawl. Does that make them
bad people?

> We will never have a better opportunity to shape another human being.

That's the wrong question. We could debate the pros and
cons of these books and a variety of other subjects from politics
to religion and never sway the people we are talking with
because they are convinced they are doing what is best for
their own family. Who can argue with that?

The point is, what standards will we set in our own house? I
am not talking about churning out little robots that think just
like us. But I am talking about providing direction, helping our
kids to focus on things that are noble, right, pure and admirable.

Our children are bombarded every day with conflicting messages. If I don't take responsibility for my girls in this area,
who will? You can be sure there will always be someone or
something ready to step right up and do our job for us, and we
may not like the results.

It is crucial that my children be guided by someone who loves
them. I do love my girls, more than life. These parenting years
are flashing by, and the opportunities to pour moral bedrock
into these kids are limited. My goal is to train up my daughters
in the way they should go (Proverbs 22:6). If that means taking
heat for being a mean mommy sometimes, so be it.

Homebodies Hint. What are some basic beliefs you want to
instill in your children? How do you plan on teaching your
kids these principles?

23

The Computer
Ate My Homework

Bending,
not breaking,
a child's will

*M*om, *I've got good news,* and I've got bad news."

"Give me the bad news first."

"The good news is—I qualified for the school spelling bee!"

I waited.

"The bad news is . . . uh . . . I got a zero on my social studies project."

"*What?*"

"Well, the computer messed up and deleted my stuff . . . "

As I listened to the millennium version of "The dog ate my homework," my temperature started rising.

"And, well, you know, I lost my rough draft . . . "

Rationalizing in a way only preteens understand, my daughter pleaded her case. The judge was not amused. The sentence: Do it again, this time for *no* credit.

"But all my stuff's at school!"

I glanced at the clock. Too late; the building was locked up.

"Then we'll go together to school first thing Monday morning, before class starts. You'll re-create your assignment while I wait."

"But the kids will make fun of me!"

(I love peer pressure, don't you?)

"That means you'll need to get it done quickly. And if it's not finished by the time school starts, I'll come back at recess. If it's not done by the end of recess, I'll come back at noon, and you'll work through lunch."

Amazingly, on Monday morning, my daughter was able to pull that assignment together, run it by me for editing and turn it in before the first bell rang.

If we could have gotten away with it, her teacher and I would have high-fived each other.

Ah . . . another benefit of being a stay-at-home mom. I can physically appear in my daughter's classroom at any time, a very effective tool when you're trying to raise responsible children.

I don't want to break her will, just bend it a little. She's a good kid, and I'm determined to do my best to keep her that way. Sure is nice to have the flexibility to do my job.

Now that both my daughters are in school all day, I have lots of discretionary time. That means I can do chores, go shopping, enjoy friends and write books like this one while Karen and Carrie soak up today's lesson across town. At the same time, I can drop those chores, shopping trips, outings and work-at-home projects on a moment's notice if something comes up where the girls need me. They are always my first priority.

I can't tell you how much I value this close-at-hand parenting. I worked in offices for almost twenty years before I came home, and I remember schedules that were sometimes so rigid, you practically had to raise your hand to go to the bathroom! It's so nice to be able to promptly tend to my children's needs, and without asking anybody else's permission to do so.

Now that I am an at-home parent, my schedule can flex to accommodate my children. Tell me my daughter is gifted in athletics or some field of study, and I can shuffle my family's activities, make appointments for special programs and drive her wherever she needs to be, sticking around to cheer her on.

Or take it the other way. A teacher calls, reporting that my preschooler has just whacked a classmate with her Etch-A-Sketch. In my old life the call would have reached me at the office, where I was committed to stay until five o'clock. By the time I'm standing in the daycare, waving my finger in her face, neither my daughter nor her now-best buddy even remember that morning's blow-up. Trying to properly chastise for something that happened so long ago is frustrating for everyone.

Timely discipline is powerful in the hands of an involved parent.

Tell me my daughter is acting up now, and I'm there like a chicken on a June bug. Since I'm nearby and freed up, I'm immediately empowered to correct, redirect or punish the offense. Timely discipline is powerful in the hands of an involved parent.

As I said before, it is not my goal to intimidate my children or to break their spirit. But for the next few years I'm their primary guide as they make their way through life. God says he disciplines those he loves, and under his tender leadership, I'm determined to do the same.

Homebodies Hint. Take advantage of the gift of accessibility. Keep a close eye on your children as they make their choices, disciplining and praising them as the moment decrees.

24

So Sue Me!

Handling sibling rivalry

I *t's a good thing you have to be* over ten years old to be a lawyer.

If it were up to my kids, everything from eating the last donut to inching across that imaginary territorial line in the backseat would be a capital offense, punishable by death.

"Did not!"

"Did too!"

"Did *not!*"

"Did *too!*"

Push.

Slug.

Body slam.

"Mom!"

They drive me nuts. And now that I'm a stay-at-home mom, I get to sort out these squabbles all day long.

Where are those want ads?

I have to admit, when we were kids, my two brothers and I often dog-piled on top of each other with fists flying. It was usually over something earth-shattering like, "He won't stop looking at me!"

Now it is my kids tussling over who sits next to daddy in the restaurant. I wonder how my own parents kept from running away from home.

Recently I told Karen and Carrie that they could have some cheese popcorn before they went to bed. Off they ran to the kitchen. An instant later they raced back down the hall, screeching and banging against the walls, each trying to reach me first.

"What's the problem, girls?"

"I want the blue bowl. She had the blue bowl last time."

"Huh, uh! *She* had it last time!"

So take the red bowl, I reasonably suggested. It is the same size, same make, holds the same amount of popcorn.

"But I *want* the *blue* one!" And with that, one daughter went wailing off into the night as the other gripped her plastic prize triumphantly.

I have learned another rule of parenting. Buy only blue bowls. I tack this truth to my long list of things they didn't mention in *What to Expect When You're Expecting.*

The worst day at home still beats the best day at the office.

Where does this domination frenzy come from? I no longer feel the need to tackle my brother Jim or whack my other brother, Rob, upside the head, so I'm happy to say most of us outgrow it.

But what do you do as a parent, while you're waiting for your kids to realize there are other more civilized ways to handle conflict?

I doubt if head-butting can be completely overcome, but we can minimize the number of run-ins. I think I handled that popcorn thing incorrectly. Instead of allowing one child to win, I should have taken away the prize. No popcorn tonight. That way, my bright children learn conflict breeds hunger.

Math and history are favorite subjects with youngsters, even before they get into school. They can tell you who got to do what, how many times, when and where. Maybe we parents can work this to our advantage.

For instance, let's use their souped-up fairness sensitivity to get children to police themselves. Consistency is the key. If Child A rode in front last time, Child B rides in front this time. Any swapping is done only by following predefined guidelines, written in blood.

I just thought of a great use for my old Day-Timer! Carrie opens the mailbox on Mondays, Karen gets first cereal pick on Tuesdays. Carrie loads the dishwasher; Karen unloads it. I'm going to schedule in some time-outs for me right now too.

Surprise—staying at home isn't always wonderful. Sometimes things get downright ugly. But even with all the ups and downs, I'm convinced that the worst day at home still beats the best day at the office.

Granted, it's not quite the utopia I imagined when I was dreaming in my cubicle. Then I had visions of being at the park with my six- and two-year-olds, lying on our backs in the grass and picking animal shapes out of the fluffy white clouds above us. Or helping my girls sound out their let-

> It's not quite the utopia I imagined when I was dreaming in my cubicle.

ters and beaming at my first grader, who of course would be reading at the seventh grade level.

Instead, I'm worried about grass stains and bugs, and the girls are bonking each other with their books.

But I'm glad to be here, nonetheless. They may be ornery kids, but they're mine. And though life on the home front is not always fun, it is definitely rewarding, even on the days when I'm more referee than coach.

Guess I'd better check this chapter over one last time. My girls notice when I mention one of them more often than the other.

Homebodies Hint. What is something specific you can do to reduce the amount of squabbling between your children? Think of something besides duct tape.

25

Beyond
Barney & Blue

*Creative activities
away from the TV*

I have to admit that when I first came home, I was a little apprehensive about how my two-year-old and I would fill our days. Most of our play experience up to that point had been via instant entertainment because, frankly, that's all we used to have time for. Videos and computer games were favorites; anything where you could just flip a switch and go. My daughter and I almost never did time-intensive crafts; that's what daycare was for!

But now there weren't any childhood education majors in my life. Just me and my toddler. Hmm.

TV was my friend. I figured that between PBS, Nickelodeon, The Disney Channel and Animal Planet, I could keep my daughter in one spot for hours. And it would be no sweat to

TV was my friend.

plug her big sister in next to her when she got off the bus from school.

But that wouldn't be right.

Okay. Everyone step away from the screen and repeat after me: That *wouldn't* be right!

You had me worried there for a second.

There is a lot to be said for educational TV, but believe me, there *is* life beyond Barney and Blue. Let's go find it.

Amanda Formaro, the Craft Corner columnist at the Homebodies website, also runs The Family Corner website. "As a mother of four children, from toddler to elementary age, I needed to find some cool crafts for the kids, but on a limited budget," Amanda says. "Craft supply stores are great and I'm like a kid in a candy store in them, but they are very pricey."

With that in mind, Amanda came up with a dozen fun projects you can make with recycled materials from around the house.

Alphabet catalog collage. Using old toy, clothing and plant catalogs, have the kids cut out colorful pictures that begin with a specific letter of the alphabet. Assign different letters to each child. Have them glue the pictures onto a piece of construction paper. Discuss the pictures afterward.

Animal jumble. Using construction or white paper, ask each child to draw a different body part of an animal, but have their animal be a secret. For example, have one child draw the head, another draw the tail, another the legs, and so on. Let the children pick the animal they want to draw. When they are done, have them put the animal together with tape or glue. Have fun coming up with a name for the animal (monk-dog-lion-potamus).

Coffee can stilts. Using two one-pound coffee cans, turn each can upside down so that the plastic lid is on the bottom. With a screwdriver, poke two holes, one on each side of the can. Using some rope or several strands of yarn braided or twisted together, thread through holes in cans. Tie off inside the can. Slip the yarn over their shoes and let them stomp around outside. Cans can be decorated if you like.

Magazine house. Cut out pictures of chairs, tables, curtains, bathroom fixtures and other furnishings from an old catalog or magazine. Spread out a newspaper or large sheet of drawing paper. Sketch an open-sided house. Have children place the pictures of the furnishings in the rooms of their choice. They can cut out more pictures to redecorate their house—pictures of people, toys, pets, anything they like!

Milk jug bird feeders. Rinse out an empty plastic gallon milk jug with lid. Cut a window in the front of the jug, and make two small poke holes for the perches. Insert pencils for perches and fill the bottom of the jug with bird seed.

Number fun. Pick a number from one to ten. Write it on a piece of paper. Ask the children to draw sets of things in that number. If the child gets number four, have them draw four apples, four trees, four dogs and so on. Have them color their pictures with crayons and markers.

Paper plate aquarium. Color an underwater scene on the "eating" side of a paper plate. Glue goldfish crackers to the scene, add a couple pieces of plastic plant for seaweed, and using glue and a little sand or soft dirt, make the sea floor. Using a second paper plate, cut a circle in the middle. Cut a circle of blue plastic wrap one inch in diameter larger than your hole in the plate. On the "eating" side of this plate, glue the blue plastic wrap so that it covers and overlaps the hole on the plate. Glue or staple both plates together with "eating" sides toward the inside. Punch a hole in the top and string a piece of yarn through the hole to hang your aquarium from the ceiling.

Paper plate holders. Using two paper plates, cut one plate in half and place on top of the other plate (turn the half plate to form a pocket over the whole plate). Use a paper punch to make holes going around the outside of the plate. Use scraps of yarn and "sew" through the holes of the plate. Start and end at the top of the plate so that it can be extended about six inches and tied. Have your children color, paint or decorate their plates. Now they have their very own place to put prized possessions, notes from mom and dad, special pictures and more.

Paper towel rain makers. Young kids love noise makers. Color, paint and decorate paper towel rolls. Cover one end of a paper towel roll with waxed paper and close it off with a rubber band. Pour a handful or two of dried beans (split peas work well) in the open end; close open end the same as the other. Poke toothpicks through the rolls at different intervals to add a "rain shaker" sound.

Pet rocks. Find smooth, flat or round rocks. Be sure to clean off any dirt or sand and dry completely before starting. Paint with acrylic paints. Decorate faces by using googly eyes, yarn for hair, markers, glitter and any other tidbits you like.

Shadowboxes. Paint the inside of a shoebox with black or dark blue poster or acrylic paint. Alternatively, you can glue black construction paper inside the box. Using white crayons or stickers, make a night scene with stars and the moon on the black background. Use small plastic toys to create a scene inside your shadowbox, or make your own with construction paper and glue. Cut out small pictures from coloring books and color and adhere to your scene. Hang a spaceship or shooting star with a piece of string and glue.

Treasure shoe box. Decorate an old shoe box and lid with construction paper, markers, paint, glue and glitter, crayons, stickers, lace, doilies or whatever else you can find. Be sure to put the child's name inside the lid. This makes a great box for treasures found out in the yard, on the way home from the park or anywhere else your children "hunt."

Thanks, Amanda! Even though my two-year-old is now a second grader, I bet she'd still enjoy a lot of these activities. Now, where's my glue?

Put your creativity in action!

I bet you'll like flipping through craft books and playing games other mothers suggest. But don't forget to tap into your creativity, devising ideas tailor-made for your own kids. Fun times like these spark children's imaginations, educate them and make memories you'll all cherish.

Homebodies Hint. Get off the couch and into the playroom! Have fun with some hands-on projects, starting with some Amanda suggested.

26

I'm Still Here

*How older children benefit
from having a
stay-at-home parent*

I need some advice from the ladies with school-aged kids," writes J.J., who is feeling blue about her baby growing up. "I love being home with my toddler and sharing all those beautiful little moments with him. Maybe I am just being emotional, but I dread the day when he no longer wants to curl up in my lap for a story. These past two years have just flown by, and I am so aware that in just three short years, he will be at school.

"I guess what I am trying to ask is, how has your life changed as you progressed from being 'mommy' to 'mom'? What are the little special moments now? Do you ever long to rock your baby to sleep, or miss bath times and wagon rides on sunny days?

"Please help me gain a better perspective of motherhood for the long haul!"

It is true, J.J., that the days of rocking my long-legged preteen are pretty much over. We try it sometimes for fun, but she crushes my lap. My back goes out just thinking about pulling her around in a

> "How does your life change as you progress from being mommy to mom?"

wagon. And I have to admit that I am relieved to not have to fight with her wet, tangled hair any more.

But we are still good about giving each other hugs, I ferry her around in the car, and she likes it when I compliment her looks. I wouldn't worry too much about your son growing up. No matter how old kids are, each stage holds its own rewards. My mom still likes me a lot, and I am in my forties!

Just as there is no time limit on enjoying your kids, don't let age be the deciding factor on whether you will stay home with them or not. Her daughter was already five when Florida mom Carole decided to become an at-home parent. "Many people tried to tell me that it was too late, that she would be in school soon and wouldn't need me at home. Hogwash!

"I have too many friends whose kids are in after-school care until 5:30 or 6:00 p.m. They get home at 6:00–6:30 p.m. Then there is dinner, baths, homework, time with family and then bed at around 10:00–10:30 p.m. No way—not my kid! I plan to be there when she gets home from school at 3:00 p.m. so homework can be done before dinner, and we have time to be a family and still get to bed at a decent hour."

I once did a live radio show where the working mother of a seventeen-year-old called in. "I've only got this last year with him. Would I be crazy to stay home now?" Not at all, I assured her. Think of the impression she would make. Can you imagine the personal value he would feel, knowing his mother loved him so much? It is an act he would remember for the rest of his life.

"I still feel the need to be at home."

Patricia Chadwick writes a teen parenting column on the Homebodies website and hosts her own website, Parents and Teens. Obviously she sees the benefit in staying home with older children. I asked her to share with us her *Top Five Reasons I Stay Home with My Teens:*

1. *To be available to my teens.* When they are home sick, I want to be there to take care of them. I don't want them to have to fend for themselves. I want to take them places and pick them up and be there when they get home from school. I want to be able to attend their events and games without working their schedules around a job.

2. *To pay attention to my teens* and know what is going on in their lives. Sometimes as a work-at-home mom, I get caught up in my own business and get too busy. But that doesn't happen routinely, and it's easier to get back to being a mom when you are your own boss, instead of explaining it to an employer.

3. *To protect my teens.* When I was a teen, the kids I tended to get into mischief with were those whose parents weren't home after school.

4. *To teach my teens.* I've always been a firm believer that it is the parent's responsibility to teach theology, doctrine, and the great truths of God to their kids. I've done this actively since my kids were little and continue into their teens. Staying at home gives me time to concentrate on this.

5. *To honor my Lord.* God called me to be a stay-at-home mom many years ago, and he hasn't relieved me yet.

As Karen enters her teens, I can relate with all the reasons Patricia listed. When I first came home, Karen and Carrie were six and two. I planned on taking a job outside the home when Carrie started kindergarten. But here I am, several years beyond that point, and I still feel the need to be at home with my girls. Honestly, I love this lifestyle so much, I may never go back into the traditional workforce, even after both kids leave home. Who knows? I may start a future support group for stay-at-home grandmas!

Homebodies Hint. Don't let age be the deciding factor in your decision to stay home. Instead, look at your individual family situation, and make choices based on that.

27

Blending Families

*How an at-home parent
eases remarriage transition*

When remarriage creates a blended family, you can assume there will be some tough kinks to work through as kids and parents establish their roles within the new home. One of the main keys to resolving conflict is spending time together, gently communicating needs and responsibilities. Having an at-home parent can help ease the transition.

Often children are emotionally wary after experiencing the heartache and trauma that precedes and accompanies a death or divorce. When Fawn, a former teacher, married Charlie, he had residential custody of his four children, ages twelve, ten, eight and four. "When you're the new mom," Fawn says, "you're dealing with all the baggage from the previous mar-

riage and the healing of the children." She
wanted to create a safe atmosphere, and
being an at-home parent helped her do
that. "I focused on making our home a positive environment, with nice music and
things that encouraged me too. I was able
to attend their games, bake them cookies

Having an at-home parent can help smooth the transition.

and be a room mother in their classrooms. We did a lot of
things together, family-bonding things. I don't think I would
have had the energy or focus to do that if I was still teaching,
with the responsibilities of grading papers, classroom planning and getting ready for the next day."

Before Fawn and Charlie were married, care for the children was shared by in-home nannies, their uncle, grandpar-
ents and special friends. Fawn would watch the kids at night
when their dad had a meeting to go to. She remembers, "The
three-year-old was always asking, 'Who is going to be taking
care of me?' or 'Who is going to watch us?' The kids really
wanted to know who was going to be there for them." As a
stay-at-home mom she was able to lend the security and balance they craved.

Fawn suggests that in a newly blended family, "Don't expect
to get anything back from the children emotionally for a long
time. It's a training situation. Your husband is a key player in
this, by the way. Through his example, he can teach them to be
thankful and respectful for what you do."

As Fawn points out, Charlie's support was vital. "I had dou-
ble the time (the birth parents) did with the kids, because he
was at work and she saw them every other weekend." This
could be good (lots of opportunities to help heal hearts) or bad
(when tempers flared). "At times I received displaced anger,
because I was there," Fawn says. "Sometimes I felt like,

'Hey—they got divorced and I got the kids!'

"But when we got married, I married all

A
stay-at-home
mom lends
the security
and balance
children
crave.

five of them. It's nice to have someone at
home now who does love their father, who
affirms him and is positive about what he's
doing, to show them his good qualities."

Fawn rejects all the "step" and "real"
references. "That breaks down the family, when you're trying
to promote unity and fairness. If I had looked at them as my
'step-children,' I would not have been able to function as well
as a stay-at-home mom. So, I can cook all their meals, do their
laundry, go to all their events and raise them, but I'm not their
'real' mother." Forget that! "I didn't birth my husband, but I
still love him with all my heart." She feels the same way about
her kids, including the two she and Charlie conceived since
their marriage.

"Charlie feels secure because he knows I love them and
want to do what is best for them," Fawn says. The couple knew
that the potential for conflict in a divorced home was high, so
they were careful to present a united front to the children. "I
called him at work, and he checked in throughout the day and
came home for lunch. It was a joint venture, with both of us
working hard on discipline and bonding."

Don't assume that all parenting clashes can be traced back
to the remarriage. "Remember that it's a natural progression
of a child to have problems as they go through their life. Sometimes, we make the excuse so we don't have to deal with it as
an instructive parent." Instead, make good use of your flexibility as an at-home parent. "The teachable moments don't
always fall during the three hours before and after work,"
Fawn notes. "We've spent hours and hours talking when the
kids were mad, when they were upset, when they were

happy—through the whole range of emotions."

Just as God expanded his family to lovingly make room for the Gentiles as well as the Jews, remarried at-home parents have a unique opportunity to help create a haven for their own blended family.

Homebodies Hint. If you're in a blended family situation, how could having an at-home parent on the scene help ease your evolution from two families to one?

PART 5

Exploring
Their Education Choices

*"We are fortunate to have
so many educational choices.
But the true blessing will come
when we match the individual child
to the teaching mode
that fits them best,
then enjoy the resulting
surge in learning."*

28

Public, Private or Homeschooling?

Choosing the best option for your family

*K*aren's first experience with public school lasted exactly three weeks. That is how long it took to transform my impressionable little redhead into a wise-cracking, profanity-spewing kindergartner.

Horrified, I yanked her out, transplanting her to a private Christian school. Still easily influenced, Karen dropped the cussing and instead began quoting Bible verses. This option worked well for three years and was so important to us that we continued paying tuition, even after I quit my job to stay home.

As Terry and I continued to feel the squeeze on our checkbook, we reevaluated our reasons for placing Karen in private school. Basically it was so she would be taught according to our beliefs. Now that I was a stay-at-home mom, I could flex

my schedule to make time for homeschooling. So as Karen finished up second grade, I started looking at curriculum catalogs. I joined a homeschooling support group, learned the laws
for my state, bought materials and prepared to start teaching
Karen myself that fall.

Two weeks before classes began, my girlfriend Robin called.
She was supportive of my decision to homeschool but wanted
me to be aware of all my options. "Have you checked out the
public school lately?" Immediately my guard went up. There
was no way I was sending my lamb to the wolves again!

But there had been positive changes throughout the local
school system during the years Karen had been in private
school. Now the principal at her public school and many of the
teachers were Christians. Robin was the head room mother
over Karen's grade, and we could request that her daughter,
one of Karen's best friends, be in the same class. "The principal, the teacher, the head room mother and a friendly classmate all sharing your family's beliefs—you will never find a
better setup in public school than this," Robin said.

She was right. So after Terry and I met with the principal
and shared our concerns, we decided to give it a try. Stashing
my third grade curriculum in a closet, ready to grab it at the
first sign of anarchy, I sent Karen off to public school—where
both her attitude and grades flourished.

That was five years ago. Every spring our family discusses
how Karen, and now her little sister, Carrie, will be taught the
coming year. So far, they're both doing great at our local public
schools. But we take it year by year, always ready and willing
to make a switch, if one is called for.

How do I know if a change is necessary? Being at home
allows me to keep close tabs on what's happening and to
actively participate in my daughters' classrooms. Shauna, who

taught in public schools for several years before becoming an at-home mom herself, says, "I am a strong believer in parental involvement and taking full charge of your child's education. As a former teacher, it always bothered me how many parents seemed to drop their kids at the door and say, 'Okay, here he is. Now fill his head with everything he needs to know, and send him home when you're done.'"

Knowing the teachers and volunteering in the classroom is essential. But it is also crucial to match the individual child to his or her optimum learning environment.

> **Knowing your child's teachers and volunteering in the classroom is essential.**

"Years ago, my parents pulled my nine-year-old sister, Stephanie, out of a Christian school where she was having social problems," remembers Christin, a former educator who now writes children's books. "I had already graduated from high school and had recently spent two weeks visiting my aunt, who was having a wonderful experience homeschooling both of her children. My parents and I discussed the situation and decided that I would homeschool Stephanie for the remainder of her fourth-grade school year. It was a really positive experience for both of us.

"Later I became a teacher. I spent seven years working with hundreds of children and their families at a variety of grade levels. Often when a child was having trouble, I met with the parents to talk about other options. I really believe that there's not one 'right' way to educate your kids. Every child has different needs. Plus, some things work for a season, then you switch to something else. The important thing is to help your child learn, and love it!"

Homeschooling can be a rewarding choice for both parent and child, but Christin cautions that it is not for everyone.

| The important thing is to help your child learn, and love it! |

"One of the biggest questions, right up there with 'What does my kid need?' is 'Am I cut out to homeschool?' Some moms don't have the temperament, organizational skills or family lifestyle that is necessary. Some have personality clashes with their kids that make homeschooling a nightmare. At the Christian school where I taught, we frequently got new students that were hopelessly behind and terribly frustrated after a failed attempt at homeschooling.

"It can be great!" Christin says. "But I think you have to be called by God to do it, and rely on him constantly for strength, wisdom and direction."

We are fortunate to have so many educational choices. But the true blessing will come when we match the individual child to the teaching mode that fits them best, then enjoy the resulting surge in learning.

Homebodies Hint. Instead of automatically reenrolling your child in the same place as last year, review available learning options. Should any changes be made?

29

Homeschooling Hurdles

Tackling some common concerns

*O*nce it is chosen, homeschooling, like any other endeavor, has its ups and downs.

"My main concern about homeschooling isn't the lack of socialization," says Carol, who is debating whether to send her child to private school in Mississippi or teach him herself. Instead she is worried that he'll be too sheltered. "He will miss the classroom and playground situations that help teach children how to deal with life and people. I am very concerned that my son will be too naïve, and my husband says school will help toughen him up."

Kass encourages Carol to take a different view. "For my son, I'd rather be the one teaching him how to handle arguments, differences of opinion, bullies and such than to have him learn it on his own or from his peers. I am very glad that I'm nearby to guide him with learning the appropriate responses and behaviors in dealing with complicated and even everyday situations."

Another roadblock some homeschooling parents run into is lack of family support. "I thought that my relatives would come around," says Pam, who is teaching her six-year-old son at home. "But all except my mom have either disapproved or said nothing and then let something slip to show their true feelings. ('Won't you be glad when your mommy lets you go to real school and play with the other kids?')

"In talking with other homeschoolers, I've found that there will always be family members who think you've lost your mind," she acknowledges. "I guess you just have to deal with each person and incident as they arise. I've decided that I'm not arguing the point or trying to convince anyone anymore. If they change their attitudes, that's great. But I don't feel that the Lord called me to convert the world to homeschooling. I know my kids better than anyone else. I'll do what God has led me to do. The safest and best place in the world is in the center of his will."

> "Won't you be glad when your mommy lets you go to real school?"

Homeschooling is legal throughout America, but regulatory laws vary, so it is critical to know your specific state guidelines. Getting involved in a local homeschooling support group will help you keep tabs on changing regulations and provide a network of friends who have made the same educational choices.

"I think every single homeschooling family I've ever met has been more than happy to share what they know with others," says Tori, an Ohio homeschooler. She tries to ease worries

of new homeschoolers who may feel overwhelmed with all the perceived rules and
regulations. "You do not have to have little
desks, a dedicated schoolroom and lesson
plans for five to six hours a day!"

Know your specific state guidelines.

Instead, many teaching experiences are
woven into everyday activities, like going
to the grocery store (math and economics), hiking in the woods
(science and nature) and seeing a movie (literature and the-
atre). Some parents do set aside a special schooling area; kids
can work just as easily at the kitchen table. And though the
state requires a set number of schooling hours per year, each
family uses their discretion in establishing a schedule. (For
instance, starting school at ten a.m. instead of eight a.m., or
teaching every other day instead of five days straight.)

What about choosing curriculum? "There are tons of homeschooling materials available, and to be a wise steward of your
money, you need to come to some decisions about things," Tori
advises. "Deciding what to buy depends on why you're homeschooling, your personal teaching style and the way your kids
learn.

"My biggest reason for homeschooling was to have control
over what they learned and how they learned it. I wanted
them to be taught subjects within a biblical context and frame-
work. That obviously affected the materials I chose.

"Some folks homeschool because they have kids that don't fit
the norm and have trouble in school—either they are brighter
and need more information faster, or they are a tad slower in a
couple of areas and need more one-on-one. Or perhaps they
have a special needs child. Therefore," Tori says, "my advice is
to articulate *why*, then go on from there. Your decision will
eliminate a fair amount of the available curriculum."

Authors Dan and Elizabeth Hamilton have compiled an extensive resource section in their book *Should I Home School?* (InterVarsity Press, 1997), listing hundreds of books, newsletters, curriculum and software vendors, organizations and homeschooling support groups.

Homebodies Hint. Do you suspect God is calling you to homeschool but still feel apprehensive? Are you already homeschooling, but have some questions or concerns? Start checking out some of the great resources available both online and in print, and visit a local homeschooling group to see how they do things.

30

Classroom Helping Hands

Volunteering at your child's school

O*ne benefit of being a stay-at-home mom* is having the flexibility to become more involved in our children's classrooms. But before you dive in, scope out the situation and see where you can be most effective.

I remember thinking that in order to be a good homeroom parent, I needed to be able to bake elaborate cutout cookies and fashion presentation-quality table decorations from doilies, glue and glitter. Since I hate to bake and have no artsy-crafty skills whatsoever, I began to dread the periodic calls for volunteers.

That is, until I learned a fundamental rule of parent participation: There's only one teacher, and there are twenty-plus sets of parents. The teacher doesn't have time to discover our hidden talents. It is up to us to let the teacher know where we would best fit in.

I am a communicator, so instead of me bringing in some burnt-around-the-edges cookies or donuts I bought at the grocery store, I should volunteer as a storyteller or a whip-'em-into-a-frenzy game coordinator.

However, I know a mom who can put together four loaves of the best banana bread you ever tasted in no time and present it with a flourish. She loves to cook, and she should let the teacher know it. There's the cookie lady!

Then there is the woman who used to work at Hallmark and does amazing things with construction paper, scissors and a glue stick. She is a perfect candidate for the bulletin board or party decoration committee.

Volunteering is fun, once you know where you fit.

There are lots of ways a parent can participate in their child's classroom activities. Explore the various opportunities available to you. Not only is volunteering fun once you know where you fit, but it also lifts your child's self esteem to see you care enough to appear regularly at their school events. Merrie has a flair for design and loves to create costumes for her four children, even though the effort can trash her home. "While they turned out really cute, I looked around at my messy house at midnight one night after hot gluing four hundred feathers on cardboard wings, and wondered why on earth I do these things.

"Then I went to my kids' class party and saw the few children who had nothing to wear and whose moms never show up. They couldn't get enough attention from me and the other moms, and even acted up to get it," Merrie remembers. "It was obvious they felt left out. My kids, on the other hand, got lots of compliments and felt like they fit in. They had a good time."

Robin has been a room mother for more than ten years, following each of her three daughters through elementary school. "Merrie is so right. The kids love it when their parents are there, and they are so proud to say, 'This is my mom!'

"One of the reasons why I like to volunteer is it allows me to get to know my kids' classmates while I make friends with the other parent volunteers," Robin says. "I think it is important to know who your kids hang out with. You get to meet the teachers, the janitors, the lunchroom ladies, the principal. You feel a little more attached, and that's a definite perk."

She acknowledges that some parents may be a little shy about volunteering, especially if they initially don't know anyone at the school. "You can always talk to the teacher and find out where to get involved. The library may need help stocking books, the lunchroom may need monitors, talent shows may need judges, or you can man booths at the school carnivals. You can work in the art room, cutting out bulletin board things for all the teachers. Or you can even go up and volunteer in the school office."

If a call for volunteers comes at a bad time, be gentle yet straightforward—you won't be able to help out this time. Keep a copy of the upcoming events schedule handy so you can say something like, "Christmas is really busy for me, but go ahead and put me down for the Valentine's party." (Note: For those tempted to do *everything*, please read chapter thirty-eight!)

Find your niche, then jump right in. Your child and his or her teacher will love you for it. Be sure to volunteer for the daytime openings first, giving working moms a chance to help out with evening activities.

Find your niche, then jump right in.

Pinpointed volunteering—matching your individual gifts to specific scholastic needs—promises a win-win-win situation for parent, child and teacher.

Homebodies Hint. Take a look at the upcoming school calendar and choose an event you would like to participate in. Then call your child's teacher and volunteer, offering your unique skills and abilities to help make the occasion a success.

31

Surviving the Last First Day of School

Facing the end of a parenting era

*K*ids grow, and we gradually learn to let go. Separations can be especially tough on stay-at-home moms, who have grown accustomed to having their babies around them throughout the day. Kindergarten was a tough hurdle for me, and I know a lot of you can relate to the emotions reflected in the following story about sending my youngest off to school.

My five-year-old's eyes shine as she moves down the aisle, shopping basket in hand. "Tweety pencils! Mommy, can I have those, please?" Carrie stretches up and points at a colorful pack hanging above her head. Plucking them from the hook, I add the No. 2s to her growing pile of school supplies.

She is delighted, and I am depressed. No, not depressed ... nostalgic. No, not nostalgic ... well, I don't know what I am.

She's delighted and I'm depressed.

My mixed-up emotions are tumbling over each other as I purchase kindergarten things for the last time, clutching a well-read elementary school supply list.

The first time I bought special pencils was several years ago, when Carrie's big sister, Karen, started school. She had the same excited glow as we moved up and down the aisle, picking out packs of construction paper and selecting just the right lunchbox.

Now Karen advises her little sister, and they move ahead of me down the row, checking out all the glittering new paints and glues, bright rulers and scissors. They are moving away, farther and farther, then disappear around the corner. My babies are gone.

Oh, stop it! I mentally slap myself for being such a weenie. What? You want them to stay home your whole life? Get a grip! Growing up is good.

I will be okay once she is actually getting on the bus every day, grinning and waving as the yellow tank rattles and grinds its gears on down the block. It might actually be nice to have some breathing time to myself, running errands without a stroller or a kleptomaniac grabbing goodies off shelves.

Yes, this could be good.

I am not unique, and the emotions I am feeling aren't limited to mothers whose babies are starting kindergarten. As I talk with friends, they give me a peek at a future they are already living. In a couple of years I will be sitting in an auditorium, watching my eldest girl's elementary graduation ceremony as she makes the transition to junior high. Then before I know it, we will be picking out a secondhand car and she will be off to college.

Bob Carlisle's "Butterfly Kisses" is sing-songing its way through my head right now. I'm gonna be a mess!

But I can't hold onto these downer emotions when I see the anticipation shining in my daughters' eyes. The kids yearn to cross those thresholds and break another boundary. I will have to learn to adjust. To let them run ahead of me, but not away from me. To change the way I relate to them without assuming there will come a day when I can't relate at all. I love them too much to let go and too much to hold on. Where is the balance?

> I'll let them run ahead of me, but not away from me.

Experts say it over and over, and I believe it is true. The secret lies in communication between parent and child. Now that Carrie is starting kindergarten, I need to step up my involvement in school, both with her and Karen. That means never missing a milestone if it is within my power to be there. I'll be more dependable than the mailman—no rain, hail, sleet or snow will keep me away.

No boss, deadline or work presentation will take precedence over my children's heart-held events. The "student of the week" spotlight . . . the choir solo . . . the spelling bee competition—all mean the world to them and so should also be precious to me.

I am not talking about paper awards here. When my children see me smiling in the crowd or across the classroom, they know they have scored high marks with their mom no matter how they perform before their peers. What a confidence builder for the child and for the parent!

Snoopy is on Carrie's backpack now instead of on her nightlight. He is evolving, adapting to a different but still important role in this little girl's world. I guess I will have to adapt too.

So go ahead and get on that bus, little one. You are not

riding off into the sunset, just into the schoolyard. I won't be far behind. You can count on me to keep you in sight and in my heart.

Homebodies Hint. Has your child recently experienced a growth spurt, either physically or emotionally? Jot down some of your observations of this exciting transitional time.

PART 6

Gaining Your
Spouse's Support

*"Mutual respect is essential,
and I must say that it is a wise man
who recognizes the immense worth
of a woman who desires
to focus her energies on nurturing
him and his children,
especially in a world that encourages
her daily to do just the opposite."*

32

A Kept Woman

Equitable division of money & respect

*H*ow did stay-at-home moms ever get labeled as helpless little women, totally dependent upon their husbands for every need or nickel? Or worse, kept women who drain their spouses dry by taking their money, but never contributing any bucks to the budget?

People may not come right out and say it, but there is a general perception that stay-at-home moms don't pull their weight financially. Of course, there are some who *do* just come right out and say it.

"There were just a few weeks before my last day of work, so I was excited and thought I'd tell my sister-in-law my good news," remembers Stephanie. "She stared blankly at me and said, 'I want to give my children every advantage, so sitting at home all day isn't for me.'

"A few months later she came over to my house with her children," Stephanie continues. "I was giving the boys haircuts and
she said, 'Oh, could you cut my son's hair too?' While I was cutting, my sister-in-law says, 'You're pretty good at this. You should
start a business called Boys' Haircuts and charge $10 per cut so
you can start contributing to your household budget again.'"

Julie was still pregnant when her father-in-law asked
where the baby was going to stay when she went back to work.
"When we told him I was going to stay home for as long as we
could financially afford it, he said, 'Well, you're going to have
to go to work at some point!'"

The pregnant wife of her husband's coworker was similarly
supportive. "She said she was only going to be able to stay
home for about two or three months," Julie said. "Our husbands work at the same place, and each has to work mandatory
overtime. I told her that for me to be a stay-at-home mom, we
had to be very creative with our finances, but it was worth it.
Then came the jab—she said that she thought it would be self-
ish of her to stay home when her husband would have to work
overtime to keep them afloat. Mind you, his job requires it!"

With unsettling stories like these, it is
no surprise some prospective stay-at-home
mothers wonder if they have any legitimate claim to the family checkbook.

**Do I
have a
legitimate
claim to the
checkbook?**

"After many months of deliberation it
has been decided that I will quit my job of
eight years to raise my two beautiful
girls," says Elizabeth, whose children are
five and two. "My husband and I are extremely happy and
enthusiastic about this change, and we both know that it will
improve the quality of all our lives, but I need a little advice.

"My husband and I have been married for nine years and have both always worked," she continues. "We are best friends, and there have never been any power trips between us. We are going to have a date soon to discuss how this new plan will work.

"My question is this: How do we balance chores, spending money/allowances and that sort of thing, without either of us feeling resentful? Should there be a percentage of his income that is an even allowance for each of us, or is it true that he earns the money, and I get what he gives me? (Please don't say the latter!)"

Money issues can constitute a huge stumbling block for any couple, whether the wife works or not. So it is vitally important that you and your husband understand and support each other in this area.

Terry and I view his paycheck as belonging to the entire family, not just him. Yes, he is the only one being paid, but he is not the only one working.

> Paychecks belong to the entire family, not just the working spouse.

Imagine how much Terry would have to pay if I wasn't doing my part to keep our family going! Even the feminists agree that each stay-at-home mom constitutes a valuable resource. Read this quote from an article in the *Philadelphia Daily News*:

> Ms. Foundation for Women is keenly aware of the value (or lack thereof) placed on traditional women's work; i.e., occupational segregation or not seeing the home as a workplace. We know that if women who worked inside the home were compensated, they'd make at least $100,000 a year. (Quote from Kelly Parisi, communications manager for Ms. Foundation's New York office, *Philadelphia Daily News,* April 27, 2000)

Since it would be too confusing to sort out exactly how much I should be paid for each individual job I do for the family, Terry and I figure we're an equally matched team and consider the one paycheck ours, fifty-fifty.

What if your husband is the one who is joking about you "not working"?

When this subject came up on the Homebodies message boards, Tori logged in with some sage advice. "Those are the types of jokes that get old really fast. We hear them from so many folks who don't understand, and we do *not* want to hear them from the person who should always be our biggest supporter!

"If the jokes really do bother you, tell him. Tell him sweetly and gently, but firmly. Let him know how it makes you feel. He may simply be trying to be funny and have no clue as to the nerve he strikes with those comments."

I am not a kept woman. I am a vibrant, integral part of this marriage and this family. I hold an important job as an at-home mother. Terry understands this and values me, just as I value him for his role. Mutual respect is essential. It is a wise man who recognizes the immense worth of a woman who desires to focus her energies on nurturing him and his children, especially in a world that encourages her daily to do just the opposite.

 Homebodies Hint. List the different support people your husband would have to hire to replace his stay-at-home wife.

33

He Works Hard for the Money

Supporting your overtime-working spouse

*A*lthough the numbers are changing as more dads decide to get in on the act, the vast majority of at-home parents are female. That means the men are the ones who head out the door each day to do the work that brings in the paycheck that puts food on the table.

Mom may be a pro at managing that paycheck once it hits their bank account, but dad is the one who, through God's grace, provides a paycheck to manage.

To spin an old record, he works hard for the money, so you'd better treat him right.

"Wait a minute," you say. "I love my husband, and I appreciate the way he provides for us. I couldn't stay home if he wasn't willing to work the extra hours to ease the financial crunch we've experienced since I quit my job. I'm proud of him for making it possible for me to spend my days with our children, teaching them how to get along in this world, infusing them with our beliefs and heritage, raising them up right."

I'm convinced. Now when was the last time you told *him* that?

There's an initial euphoria that takes hold when we first capture our dream of becoming at-home parents. That feeling carries us through the first round of tough times, and often our marriages flourish as we stand together against obstacles.

When did you last thank your spouse for working overtime?

But time passes. We settle into a routine of focusing on the kids while our husband focuses on his job. With all our attention turned toward our cubs, we may miss those first rumblings of discontent coming from Papa Bear.

Grrrr . . . I spend less time with the kids since she came home.

Grrrr . . . How long do I have to keep this up?

Grrrr . . . I'm nothing but an unappreciated workhorse!

Roar!

Momma Bear jumps out of her skin, the cubs scatter, and the warm den flash fires with accusations and hurt feelings.

Most of the time, explosions like this are signaled long in advance of the blow-up and can be avoided by simply remembering to show our appreciation on a regular basis.

Shauna is careful to do "thoughtful little things to make home a welcome and safe haven. One thing that I try to make sure is that dinner is simmering on the stove, or something yummy is in the oven when Tom gets home. I remember as a child coming in from playing and smelling mom's cooking, and it was such a welcome aroma! My husband works hard and is often tired or stressed when he gets home. I love to hear him come in and say, 'Oh, something smells so good in here!'

"Another thing, the kids and I often just get goofy when he comes home. The other night, when we heard the garage door open, we positioned ourselves at the top of the stairs so that the moment he stepped into the house, he saw us jumping up and down and chanting: 'We love Daddy! We love Daddy! We love Daddy!' I think he really likes coming home, wondering what crazy thing we'll be doing next."

Carole shares her own strategies for making her husband feel appreciated. "The obvious ways are to make sure the house is straight, our daughter's room is straight, my attitude is straight (no matter how bad my day has been, I don't discuss it until after dinner) and dinner is cooked when he comes home.

"I also make sure he knows that this is a 'gripe-away' zone. He can say anything he wants to about work with me, because he knows it won't go any further than the front door. I don't give him advice about work unless he asks for it.

"If he calls to say he is going to work late, I don't whine or pout," Carole continues. "I put on my brightest voice (no matter how I'm really feeling) and say, 'Don't worry about it. We'll be home when you get here. Take your time, do what needs to be done, and drive home safely. Everything is under control here, so don't you worry about a thing.'

"Lastly, at least once each week I thank him for working so hard, for believing in our dream and our family enough to do all that he does."

Having an at-home parent demands teamwork, and dad appreciates recognition as much as mom does. Take time to honestly encourage and thank your spouse, as you each do your part in reaching your family-focused common goal.

 Homebodies Hint. Make a top ten list of reasons you appreciate your husband and present it to him when he gets home.

34

Daddy's Home

The challenge of being a stay-at-home dad

*T**hose who snicker at the concept* of dad staying home with the kids are out of touch with a quiet revolution going on in American society. This revolution has two major catalysts: the proliferation of personal computers and the fact that most companies are finally offering both sexes equal pay for equal work.

With many women making as much or more than their husbands, it can no longer be automatically assumed that mom will be the one who quits full-time work to raise the kids. Also, computer access has generated a tidal wave of employees, both male and female, surging from their offices to their homes.

The guys themselves may not even realize that they've crossed over into the stay-at-home dad realm. Approach a group of men at church and ask how many are at-home dads. Most likely no hands will go up. Now ask how many of them have home-based businesses or work from home for their employers and about 25 percent will say they do.

> Today's fathers demand much more time with their children.

What is it they say about a rose by any other name? The same thing happened several years ago when some women demanded to be called domestic engineers instead of homemakers. But whatever you called them, they were there when their kids needed them. And that's becoming increasingly true of today's fathers, who are demanding much more hands-on time with their children than their own fathers had.

But what about the guys who decide to forego the work-at-home position and wholeheartedly embrace a traditional full-time, at-home parenting role?

Although Eric and Carla Lapp always knew he would be the one staying home with their children, they understand their choice doesn't reflect the norm. Most couples who consider having a parent at home figure they'll both work until the baby is born, then the wife will be the one to quit her job or go on sabbatical for an extended period of time.

But that doesn't always turn out to be the best choice. Eric, who writes a column for stay-at-home dads on the Homebodies website, likes to share his impression of how that realization hits a lot of guys. Eric can hear him now, the imaginary husband who has his parenting future neatly on track, never expecting the U-turn ahead:

> Three years into our marriage my wife greets me at the door with a hug that wraps me up like a Python's first meal in a year.

"Oh, Honey, what's going on? Are you pregnant?" I exclaim.

"Uh, no, I . . . I . . . ," she stutters.

"Go ahead, Honey. You look so happy."

"I am. I got a job. It's a great job and it would make a great career for me. It kind of came out of the blue. It pays so well, I just couldn't turn it down. It is a vice president position, and I will be making twice as much as you. Isn't that great?!"

The imaginary husband drops his briefcase. He can't remember Life 101 saying anything about this. He will have to go back and check his notes.

Of course, the next week we find out we're having a baby.

Eric grins as he considers what his boyhood chums would have thought about his future at-home profession. "Try to envision this," he says.

The guys are hanging out next to the baseball diamond taking a break from a ferocious game of kickball. It's hot; it's humid; it's summertime in suburban Chicago. With cap guns in one pocket and a few packages of Pop Rocks in the other, the guys strike up a conversation.

"Ya know, if you swallow your gum it stays in your stomach for seven years," I wisely state.

Gasps of "really?" fall like dominoes down the wooden bench, paint cracked and peeling from cold winters and sweltering summer heat.

"Yea, did you guys know that this kid in Westchester died from putting too many Pop Rocks in his mouth at once? Just killed him," Bruce bellows.

More contemplative whimpers at the possibilities of such a gruesome death.

"Hey, what do you guys wanna be when you grow up?" Bruce asks.

Kevin jumps in. "The next Walter Payton. If I play football, that is. I might decide to play hockey, then I'd be a center like

Stan Makita, or maybe I'll play baseball. I dunno."

Steve says, "I'm gonna be the guy that cleans the windows on the outside of the Sears Tower."

I add proudly, "I'm going to be a stay-at-home dad!" Stunned silence. "You know, let my wife go to work and I will raise my kids and take care of the house." I look around at the dropped jaws and smirks of wonderment that would soon turn to hysterical laughter.

From the flopping bodies in the sand and dust come bullets of sarcasm.

"Hey Lapp, are you kidding me? A stay-at-home dad? You sissy."

"What a &%#@ loser."

"Lapp dog, where's your apron?"

"Hey, Mommy Lapp! Go fix me some grub!"

But Eric has had the last laugh. Instead of being caught up in a competitive workplace, he is using his unique management skills at home. His kids aren't the only ones to benefit either. Carla can confidently work outside the home knowing her three little ones, Alexis, Jacob and Nathaniel, are safe in their daddy's hands. Eric is also careful to provide a safe haven for his mate. "While a stay-at-home dad has so many roles, like teacher, house cleaner, disciplinarian, encourager, toy and house repair technician, dishwasher and owwie-kisser, just to name a few, he will always win the championship if he remembers he is first and foremost a stay-at-home husband."

Eric understands the importance of carving out time with other men too. "I just recently completed a course through the National Center for Fathering. Professional dads, don't hog all that good stuff you are learning. Be a mentor to a young or new father; hang out with a dad who is struggling; give some time to a young family that hasn't had the advantages you

Don't
call him
Mr. Mom. He
made a
parenting
choice, not a
gender swap.

have had. Just as you are making an incredible difference *inside* your home amidst the toys, diapers, strollers and books, so also you can make an impact *outside* your home on young fathers who need a role model who cares and understands."

As Eric encourages them to support each other, what are some things the rest of us can do to show at-home dads that we admire their decision to focus on their children?

Don't call them Mr. Mom. If you've got to hang a label on them, call them Mr. Dad.

Don't expect them to be effeminate. They've made a parenting choice, not a gender swap.

Respect their wives as loving parents who have chosen the best care available for their particular children.

Don't devalue them by making jokes, asking how their wives feel about them "not working" (a question that sets *all* at-home parents off) or implying that they don't have the natural parenting instincts that mothers do.

Give them credit for being trendsetters in a society that doesn't fully accept them—yet.

Homebodies Hint. Have you and your spouse been considering the at-home lifestyle for mom? Turn it around. What advantages might there be to having dad stay home instead?

PART 7

Handling Household Responsibilities

*"It's all well and good
to strive for excellence in homemaking,
but watch out for the
glittering kryptonite that threatens
many stay-at-home moms:
perfectionism in all the wrong places."*

35

Marathon Mom

A busy but blessed homemaker

*A*s I write this handbook, my daughters, at ages eight and twelve, are neither toddlers nor teens. I like to tell people that I'm in the relatively easy years, and it's true. But don't think I've forgotten what it was like when they were younger! For those who are still tackling two-foot-tall tornadoes, I say, "Hold on, Marathon Mom. It gets better, I promise!"

When my husband, Terry, proposed, he didn't use the classic "Will you marry me?" line. Instead he asked me to be the mother of his children. Misty-eyed, I agreed.

I didn't realize I had just signed up for the race of my life.

Now don't misunderstand me. I would do anything for our two jaunty little redheads. But I'm learning motherhood has a

I didn't realize I'd just signed up for the race of my life.

lot more to do with running shoes than baby booties.

The glorious days of hitting the snooze button are over. Each morning the alarm beside my bed fires off like a pistol shot.

My naive images of Madonna and child left in the dust, I'm off on a fast track unlike any I experienced in the working world. Relatives and friends cheer from the sidelines, shouting their favorite child rearing pointers and admonitions.

There are no set rules for this tough course, however. I'm going to have to figure it out as I go, as the road ahead veers with twists and turns to challenge the most determined marathon mom.

Flipping on overhead lights and whipping back bedspreads, I tickle little bottoms as my kids grope blindly for their covers. "Time for school! Let's go!"

This morning's hurdles include dressing my preschooler, Carrie, who is yelling, "I can do it myself!"—but can't—and beating my third-grader's rumbling bus to the curb. With a hurried hug and a half-zipped coat, Karen is on her way. Her sister perches expectantly at the window, then waves a pudgy hand and oatmealy spoon, splattering the TV, our cat and herself as she belts out, "Bye-bye!"

Bounding up the stairs with Carrie in tow, I dash back to their bedroom. On the floor are five or six discarded outfits that didn't make the first string. Peeling off the soiled garment, I find myself back at the starting line. Howling, "I *can do* . . . umph!" Carrie's demand is muffled as I do it myself, pulling a stubborn turtleneck over her carrot top.

As the whipping whirlwind continues to swirl, my husband is caught up in the fun too. Smoothing bedspreads and plopping breakfast dishes in the sink, Terry jogs along beside me for a while, then veers off to his own job.

Running in place, I watch him leave, wondering at the ease with which he separates the track at home from the track at work. How do guys do that? Even when I worked full time, my mommy track plotted a course right through the middle of my office.

There is no time to think of that now though. Gathering speed, I face into the headwind. Snatching various hats on and off throughout the day, I sprint through my various roles: accountant, chauffeur, cook, interior decorator, laundress, maid, physician, secretary and preschool teacher. That is just for today. Tomorrow the course will change, and so will the hats.

By the time Karen bursts in the front door with a backpack of homework and a serious case of the munchies, I'm beginning to get winded. But there is still dinner to be prepared.

Uh, oh. Mother Hubbard's cupboard is bare. Ready or not, it is time for that most thrilling of all challenges: grocery shopping with the kids.

An hour later we are back home with fast food. After streaking down aisles, rescuing teetering boxes and bottles in the wake of my two mini-tornadoes, I decide to let off the pace a bit. The local hamburger joint can do the dishes.

"Daddy! Daddy!" Karen and Carrie race to open the door as Terry's key turns in the lock. Together we sit at the kitchen table, munching fries as I don my counselor's hat. Workplace traumas, schoolyard adventures and household mishaps shared, the course finally begins to wind down.

After homework and splashed-to-the-ceiling baths, it is time for songs and books. With a kiss and snuggle-hug I tuck in each of the girls and flip off the light.

I didn't set a world record, but I ran a good race.

As I cross the finish line, the imaginary crowd fades into a peaceful contentment. I haven't set a new world record or anything like that, but I have run a good race.

Maybe I didn't realize the implications of saying "Yes" to Terry when he asked me to be the mother of his children. But I wouldn't trade my marathon for anything. Tomorrow I get to hack out a fresh course. I'm looking forward to seeing what is around that next curve.

Homebodies Hint. Think back over today's events. Which stand out as the best moments in your own marathon?

36

Super
Stay-at-Home
Mom

Workaholism begins at home

*A*sk a prospective stay-at-home mom what she hopes to accomplish by making the jump to home and you'll usually get an answer like, "I want to spend more time with my children" or "I want to nurture myself and my family." Seldom is the reason "I want to have my laundry done by three p.m." or "I'd rather flame out doing volunteer work."

But as a long-time stay-at-home mom, I still sometimes find myself tripped up by a perfectionistic mindset, embedded in the way I perceived myself when I was in the workforce. You see, I was the quintessential Super Mom, determined to be the right arm my boss had only dreamed of. *I will be the best worker the world has ever seen.*

Didn't happen. Instead, I was merely mediocre in most

> The desire was there; the necessary twenty-eight hours a day were not.

areas. The desire was there; the necessary twenty-eight hours a day were not. By the time I quit work, I was one whipped puppy, run over by excessive expectations.

Those first few months at home were wonderful. The more relaxed schedule allowed me to recuperate.

I healed.

I perked up.

I realized that not only could I do a good job as a stay-at-home mom, *I could be the best stay-at-home mom the world has ever seen.*

Enter my fiendish alter-ego, Super Stay-at-Home Mom.

Faster than a speeding guilt trip. At work my job responsibilities were clearly designated. These are your tasks, these are your deadlines. Approach your work in this manner, and you're sure to get ahead.

There is no such manual for being a stay-at-home mom. But I had a pretty good idea of what was required: sparkling floors, homemade bread, fresh-scrubbed kids and smiles . . . lots of smiles. I'd never actually met a perfect stay-at-home mom in real life, but her glossy image spurred me on—just as Super Mom had motivated me at the office.

Hard to believe I'd fall for that line again, but I did.

Let me think. To be a successful stay-at-home mom, I need to bake like Betty Crocker, sew like June Cleaver, volunteer like Mother Teresa and clean like the Scrubbing Bubbles.

Who makes up these rules? I don't know. Maybe they are the result of subliminal messages hidden in detergent commercials. Maybe they are inbred in women who believe they will succeed if they simply work harder, longer, smarter than men. Maybe they spring from an inner voice that whispers—falsely—that stay-at-home moms aren't quite as valuable as other women, but that they will succeed if they just work harder, longer, smarter than their working mother counterparts.

Whatever the motivation, it wasn't long before I realized there was something seriously wrong with this Suzie Homemaker chick I had invited into my house. My cookies were crispy, my seams sagged, and there were rings around my collar, in the bathtub and under my eyes.

Enter my fiendish alter-ego, Super Stay-at-Home Mom.

Suzie was a slave driver, and I was learning to despise her more each day.

I'm not the only one. Super Stay-at-Home Mom Syndrome sparks nightmares in many stay-at-home dream houses.

"I had all these grand goals and plans about our house, our life together, wonderful volunteer efforts, and starting a part-time business from home," says Gail, who was formerly in the engineering field. "I ran myself ragged trying to accomplish all these things in a very short period of time. And my child was interfering with all my best efforts!"

Joan, another quality-minded mom, also quickly became disillusioned: "I used to hate those magazine articles that would advise you to lower your standards: 'Ignore the dust bunnies under the bed; don't feel you have to change the bed linens every week.' Geez, I was having trouble finding enough relatively clean dishes to eat off of. Forget the dust bunnies!"

Joan's got a point. Forget the dust bunnies. Where are our kids?

There is an awful lot of work for a stay-at-home mom to do. But refocus. Why did we come home? Wait—it's coming back: We wanted whiter shirts and lemony-fresh cabinets.

Duh!

It's all well and good to strive for excellence in homemaking, but watch out for the glittering kryptonite that threatens many stay-at-home moms: perfectionism in all the wrong places.

"There's a lot more to life than what the house looks like," points out Karen, who came home with her newborn, Jessica, a little over a year ago. Karen had been very task-oriented at work and struggled at first with seeing few concrete rewards as a stay-at-home mom. But she soon realized something had to give, and that something was the unrealistic schedule she had set up for herself.

"You have to spend time on your emotional and spiritual health. You're also helping your child with their social skills, training them up so they can have good relationships."

Karen has discovered the truth behind the words "less is more." "I know I'm going overboard when I start getting irritated when Jessica needs me. That's when I say, 'Slow down, Karen. Get your priorities straight.'"

So how do we do that? Knowing why you're doing what you're doing is a good place to start.

More powerful than a loco motive. I still tend to float off track when I become project-oriented instead of little-people-oriented. This is an ongoing problem with recovering perfectionists, and I experience it as regularly as the next stickler. One thing that helps me is thinking through my motives for being home.

Did I become an at-home parent to impress others with my cleaning skills? If my goal really was to have the best manicured lawn in the neighborhood, then I guess I should drag out the John Deere and go for it. But if it was to have the best mannered kids in the neighborhood, then I shouldn't feel guilty if the grass gets a little high while I am trimming my child's tendency to grab other kid's toys.

Am I here to manhandle our finances? Uneasiness about living on one income throws Super Stay-at-Home Mom into a penny-pinching frenzy. She's so conscientious about weeding the wants from the needs that she forgets that sometimes we need a want or two.

Having a budget allows Terry and me some flexibility while preserving our ability to get by on a reduced income. Since we know where the money is going, we can clearly identify areas where we can splurge every once in a while. I am not talking about blowing a paycheck! But I do think it is important to build in a little mad money, or else the whole family will eventually fall into miser-induced burnout.

Did I quit work so I could become a slave to my family? I put myself in time-out at least once a week. That means I go off the clock, leave the house and rejuvenate with friends or by myself, doing something totally unrelated to parenting.

Super Stay-at-Home Mom demands sacrifice of self, but who really wants a martyr for a mother? Get some time away, recharge your batteries, then come back ready to nurture your little ones.

No one wants a martyr for a mother.

Being in agreement with your spouse helps block barbs from that pesky Super Stay-at-Home Mom. Who cares what *she* thinks, as long as your husband supports your efforts?

However, if Hubby is impatient about the house not being perfect or dinner not being on the table at five o'clock sharp, then he swings the door open for our fiendish alter-ego's triumphant reentry: "I'll work harder, faster, smarter . . . become the most perfect wife and mother there ever was." Or she'll flatten him with her sparkling frying pan.

Either way, it is time for a chat. Talk over your motives. Do you need to tweak your expectations a bit? If you need it, ask for help or more flexibility from your spouse.

Able to leap tall misconceptions in a single bound. Keeping those lines of communication open with my husband has been vital to the success of our at-home experiment. Over the years, sharing our feelings and ideas has helped us to weather whatever comes our way. I take life one day at a time, and having a bit of at-home experience under my belt has taught me to loosen up. For instance:

Money has been tight, but annual raises and reviews have arrived too.

I have learned to let sleeping dust bunnies lie.

Loneliness no longer looms, since I have linked up with other like-minded moms through parenting organizations, walks in the park and chatting on the Web. Via computers, e-mail and the Internet, work-at-home opportunities have sprung up too.

It is enabling, invigorating and inspiring to leave the guilt, loco motives and misperceptions behind. Super Stay-at-Home Mom can keep her stress and storm clouds. I'm learning to blend my expectations with those of my husband and my loving God, and the results—reflected in the faces of my children—look promising.

Homebodies Hint. What drives you as an at-home parent? Pinpoint unrealistic expectations held by both you and your spouse, and devise a plan for banishing Super Stay-at-Home Mom from your house.

37

Housework + Husband = Headache?

Getting help with the chores

I'm a stay-at-home mom who feels like a full-time maid," sighs Ann-Marie, a Massachusetts mother of three. "It's not that I don't like being a homemaker; I'm so glad I'm here to make a difference in the lives of our children. But I need some help!

"I know my husband works hard all day outside the home, but I don't think he fully realizes how hard it is to work *inside* the home. Sometimes I truly feel that my family thinks they live at the Holiday Inn! Is providing financially for our family enough to ask of my husband?"

If you're experiencing a similar type of how-do-we-balance-the-housework frustration, it's time to get back to basics with your spouse.

Tell me again why I quit my job. Was it to do my husband's laundry?

Did I quit my job to do my husband's laundry?

Don't get me wrong. I'll be happy to clean his clothes and do my best in tackling the daily household duties. But if I'm not mistaken, the *primary* reason I'm spending more time on the homefront is to nurture our kids with the special hands-on training only a loving parent can provide.

That means my focus will be on character first, clean floors second.

The at-home parent will naturally have more opportunities to perform chores than the spouse who's working outside the home. But that doesn't mean that our husbands get a free ride.

Now, I'm not trying to give the guys a bad rap. I don't think most husbands plan to be insensitive. And I definitely don't advocate nagging or bullying them into helping out. (That will normally backfire anyway.) As Suzie, an at-home mom from Pennsylvania, notes, "They really don't realize how much we do, till we stop doing it. My hubby got a wake up call one day when I was so sick, I couldn't move from the bed. He had to take care of everything, and when I was better (twenty-four hours later), he said he was never so glad to be able to work outside the home!

"He finally realized how much I do, day in and day out (that wasn't even including the kids I usually baby-sit). Ever since then he has been much more apt to help out. I also notice that when I don't acknowledge and praise (him for work done), he doesn't try as hard. When I am loving and appreciative, he does more!

"He has his slumps or lazy periods," Suzie acknowledges. "You know what I do then? I don't worry about much, myself. I sit down with him and be a bum too! This isn't so easy for me; it has taken some practice. I used to be very compulsive, quite the neat freak. But when I do this and just take on a carefree attitude, then I don't get angry and resentful."

"Housework is one area where my hubby shines," says Chris, whose husband, Ernest, is a stay-at-home wife's dream. "I'd like to take credit for it, but he went into our marriage with a healthy attitude about helping out around the house. It also helps that he's reinforced the idea to my kids that they should clean up their own messes as well.

"Around four p.m. each day is 'clean up time' for my kids. They fuss and moan about it, but they understand it is their duty to pick up toys and clothes that have been strewn about that day so the house looks neat and tidy by the time dad gets home. If they don't have it cleaned up by the time he arrives, there's no TV, computer, and so on, until the job is done. They also lose the reward they gain by having it clean in time.

"By the way, it did take a while for my hubby to develop realistic expectations about my level of housekeeping once I became a stay-at-home," Chris admits. "My domestic skills were never exemplary, and I had been raised with the notion (mine, mentors' or mother's—I'm not sure) that I would work a career position and hire someone to do the mundane cleaning tasks. Not so! But my lack of cleaning skills showed more once I came home full time, and were accentuated by my husband's notion that I'd have all the time in the world once I got there." As Chris and Ernest discussed what they expected from each other, the tension lifted and they settled into a cooperative cleaning routine that works well for them.

From her home in Belgium, Rosemarie chimes in with her appreciation of husbands like Ernest who require their children's help with the housekeeping. "The only men that I know who are helpful with housecleaning are those who've been well trained by their mothers. So ladies, if we want our future daughters-in-law to be grateful, let's start training our boys!"

Although helping provide a clean and comfortable home is part of an at-home parent's job description, it is by no means the defining standard. If you feel yourself morphing into, as Ann-Marie puts it, "a stereotypical shrew of a wife, yelling 'No one around here appreciates me!'" it's time to call a family meeting. Ask for help. Together reexamine expectations and redistribute the workload.

Agree on a cooperative cleaning routine.

After all, you're a stay-at-home mom, not a stay-at-home maid.

Homebodies Hint. Write down some chores you would like to have help with. Now get your family members together and talk about how you can all work together to knock out household duties.

38

Never-at-Home Moms

Overcommitment to extracurriculars

*T**he anonymous e-mail sounded familiar.* It reflected a problem encountered by many new stay-at-home parents: the perception by family and friends that we have lots of free time to help with their projects, since we no longer "work."

"When I first stayed home, I was relieved," the message read. "Now I'm everyone's babysitter, maid, taxi driver and whatever else they can think of. I have tons of people thinking that because I'm a stay-at-home mom, I should be grateful to have something to do by running their errands."

Sounds like it's time to show some gentle assertiveness! Stephanie related her own run-in with an overzealous committee organizer. "I actually turned down (politely of course) yet another request for me to take on an additional task. This is a triumph for me! I hate saying no and feel so bad when I do.

"I definitely have enough on my plate right now, so I graciously declined. You know what? She was very understanding and wasn't mad at all. To all the other 'yes girls' out there: Saying no can be painless."

People think we have lots of free time since we don't "work."

Stephanie's right. Often we are the ones putting pressure on ourselves. "In the beginning I was so excited to have options that I joined everything I could—moms' groups, MOPS, a playgroup, swimming and dancing," remembers J.J. "I finally burned out and decided to drop most things for a while. I think my son and I were both glad!"

"I am notorious for being overcommitted," admits Leanne, a North Carolina homeschooler. "I jumped head first into our local support group and was involved on the board for two years—two very long years.

"Being a board member is a lot like being a customer at a demented beauty salon. You sit down to get your nails done and instead of polishing your nails and trimming your cuticles, they start shoving bamboo up your fingernails!

"I know not all volunteer positions are like this," Leanne admits. "But it's always a sacrifice and the sacrificial lambs are usually your family. I speak from experience, unfortunately."

"Where do I start?" asks Dana. "It seems like Jeff comes home and I leave. Between watching the kids and all the church responsibilities, Sammi's dance class and traveling to see our parents, we have little time for ourselves.

"There are periods when we have to devote a lot of attention to projects or special events. I guess the thing that Jeff and I are finding out is that we need to make that time more of an exception than the norm.

"I'm sure this will always be a juggling act, because as the kids get older, their activities will increase. But I am realizing the need to not spread myself too thin, to the point of having nothing, especially physical energy, left for my family."

"I know why we do it," declares Charlotte, a Michigan mom. "Our egos are still bruised from leaving the existence-justifying work world." She sees herself and other at-home mothers trying to please imaginary coworkers, "who, in my own mind, have heaped scorn and derision on me for my slackness, my laziness of not putting career ahead of all else. Alas, it has nothing to do with my beloved child and everything to do with self-worth issues."

I suspect Charlotte is at least partly right. Low self-esteem propels many parents into the "I'll be the best volunteer they've ever seen" wing of Super Stay-at-Home Mom Syndrome. But there are plenty of people with healthy self-images who morph into never-at-home moms too.

Betsy, an Orlando, Florida, mother of three, jumped into at-home parenthood with both feet, then found she needed to step back from a lot of the attractive activities. "This SAHM thing has a definite learning curve. At first you try to do it all. Then you realize it's impossible." Eventually, Betsy says, you fall back on what should have been Plan A—determining how much you can comfortably handle, regardless of the subtle (and not so subtle) pressures of other people. "You really need to pick and choose what works best for you."

How do you know when you're maxed out? Sit in a quiet place and take an objective look at your schedule. When you examine your commitments, do you feel peace or irritation? Are some activities robbing you of your joy, instead of adding to it?

Are your activities robbing you of joy, instead of adding to it?

Also watch for signals from your family. If you're hearing lines like "I don't want you to go" from your kids or sense simmering resentment from your spouse, it's time to put on the brakes. No one is trying to tie you to the kitchen sink; there are many worthwhile volunteer efforts and fun activities that take place outside our homes. But use discretion so you don't get stretched too thin.

There is a big difference between thoughtfully deciding to do something and being drafted. Just say "no" when appropriate. Doing so enables you to truly enjoy the times you say "yes."

Homebodies Hint. If you're feeling swamped, stop taking on extracurricular duties, no matter how attractive, *now*. Finish up your present commitments, let the dust settle and take some time off. Once you've rested, you will be better able to decide exactly where to get involved without overwhelming yourself or your family.

PART 8

Sharing Your Faith

"It was only when I came to know Jesus and surrendered my whole being—my life, my desires, my everything— and made the conscious decision to have him be Lord of everything about me, that the whole world finally fell into place."

39

Latchkey Parents

Providing a safe house for neighborhood kids

*W*hen *I was growing up,* the neighborhood came alive after school. Touch football, Barbies, Chinese jump rope—the kids poured off the buses, shoving and pushing into each other's yards. Moms sat on the front stoops, talking to each other and running for salve when a set of training wheels went awry.

Now the yards are remarkably quiet as the afternoon bus rumbles up the street. My second grader won't see most of her friends until they're picked up from after-school care, once their parents get off work. My preteen's peers disappear behind locked doors, forbidden to venture out. The miracle of call waiting allows them to talk to friends, though, and our phone rings almost immediately after Karen walks in the door.

I never answer it; it's always for her.

The neighborhood is okay; it's just on simmer. It'll fire up once the working parents start pulling in their drives, with more kids spilling from cars and running to each other's houses.

But I can't help but wonder what's going on in those buildings before the cars arrive. Any illusions I had about preteens and teens no longer needing at-home parents were swept away long ago. There have been too many afternoons my own daughter has burst in the door, stormy-faced or breathless with happy news. I'm glad I've been here to hear it, good or bad, because like her daddy, my daughter tends to quickly bury her emotions. The difference between 3:30 p.m. and 5:30 p.m. is the difference between me getting the whole story or hearing "Nothing."

So what about these other preteens and teens on our street? I know there are younger kids behind those doors, too, since many families save after-school care costs by having their students come straight home.

> We've got a prime mission field in our own backyards.

At-home parents, we've got a prime mission field in our own backyards. Is God tapping you on the shoulder? Maybe you're supposed to open your doors and invite the latchkey kids in!

"Call me a stay-at-home evangelist," says Rhonda, a Lenexa, Kansas, mom who loves entertaining neighborhood kids along with her own four children. "I certainly never expected this benefit, but being a stay-at-home mom allows me time to minister to our neighbors in a way I don't think I could if I worked full time outside the home.

"I especially savor the opportunities I have to reach out to

the children and teenagers in our neighborhood. For example, a buddy of my teen-
age son asked me, 'Do you believe in
ghosts?' I surprised him when I said, 'Yes.'
Then I told him the story of King Saul, who
went to a witch to try to contact the spirit
of Samuel. The witch did indeed conjure up
a supernatural being, and the results were *not* good!

"Call me a stay-at-home evangelist."

"At other times my children's friends have asked us why we
object to certain movies and video games. I've been able to
explain our views on purity, both mental and physical, and
why we try to avoid 'the very appearance of evil.' When kids
complained that the 'Bible is boring,' I entertained them with
some of the Bible's more graphic battle stories.

"I've hauled vanloads of neighborhood youngsters to church
with me, sometimes making two trips because our Voyager
couldn't hold them all. Would I be able to do all this if I worked
outside the home?" Rhonda asks. "Maybe. I just know that, for
now, my personal mission field is right outside my door. And,
for now, it is enough."

Sometimes you're able to minister to the parents too. Chris
found an opportunity to help a young working mother who
lived in her trailer court in St. Louis, Missouri. "Her family's
total income is only about half of ours, and that's with both
parents working. She has to hitch a ride with her mother-in-
law in order to get to her job. Since her mother-in-law doesn't
have the same work schedule she does, this sometimes means
she has to leave for work before her kids get on the bus, and
once in a while their bus will get back before she does.

"I volunteered to watch her kids for her during these crunch
times," Chris says. "The kids know that if they ever come
home and Mom's not there, they're welcome to come up to my

place, and I'll help them find out where she is and keep them safe and warm until she gets home. I also help out with watching them if school is called early because of bad weather.

"I've never asked for money from her, but she has given it to me on occasion, and we've fostered a real friendship too. She has the support she needs to keep on working her day job, and my children and I get to bond with an especially sweet pair of kids."

You will have to set boundaries, of course, so your house doesn't become a free daycare dumping ground for unscrupulous parents. But don't let that minor concern keep you from reaching out to youngsters around you. Who knows how God might use you in a child's life—or their parent's?

Homebodies Hint. With so many parents working outside the home, there is a good chance there are lonely latchkey kids within shouting distance of your front porch. What can you do to foster friendliness and become known as a "safe house" within your neighborhood?

40

Training Up a Child

Raising godly children

*T*here are only two people in this world whose lives I can truly sculpt: my children, Karen and Carrie.

What about my husband, Terry? Nope. His personality, dreams and aspirations were pretty much set when I met him. I can encourage him, of course, as we travel together through our married life. But Terry came to me already assembled. Another woman—my mother-in-law, Mary—trained him up, and I'm thankful she did a good job of it.

Karen and Carrie were laid in my arms as innocents. They have their God-given personalities and a perfect plan for their lives laid out before them by their heavenly Father. My job is to raise my children, carefully nurturing, disciplining and teaching them about life and their Lord. They start out holding my hand, then I introduce them to Jesus, who gently takes their other hand. If things go the way I hope, my girls will eventually let go of me and walk securely with him for the rest of their lives.

What an awesome responsibility!

God put you in our family for a reason.

Deanne, who stayed home with her two children for fifteen years, shares Jesus as though he is in the room (which according to Scripture, he is). When her children were very young, she used simple concepts to teach them about Christ. "I told my kids, 'God loves you; God made you; God put you in our family for a reason,'" Deanne says. "I introduced them to worship songs, then went devotional book shopping, putting a lot of thought into what was age-appropriate."

As a new parent Deanne wanted her kids to be as comfortable in church as at home, so attendance was a priority. She was very strict about family devotions. "I felt it necessary to do that every day, before we did anything else. You get up, go to the bathroom, brush your teeth, do devotions. But as my children got older and I matured in my own understanding of the discipling process, it became less of a structured time and more of a lifestyle.

"When my daughter was a preschooler and she went everywhere with me, we would pray before we got into the car," Deanne remembers. "'Help us to be safe; help us to use this money wisely; help us to help others.'" Sirens signaled prayers for officers rushing to get the bad guy, or aid for the person who might be injured. "While grocery shopping, we'd buy one thing extra to give away and put it in the barrel for the hungry. I wanted to make giving a natural part of shopping, to teach her to not only think, 'What do I want?' but also, 'What do others need?'"

Like all mothers, Deanne wasn't always the best model. "It's easy to get a devotional and make your kids listen as you read it, make them repeat a prayer or parrot a verse," she says. "What's hard is living an honest, open, ever-evolving spiritual life before your children, who are witnesses to your best and worst moments. If I sin in front of them, it's crucial for me to repent in front of them too."

As Dr. James Dobson of Focus on the Family states so well, parenting isn't for cowards. But here is some good news: it isn't a solitary venture either. To paraphrase Jesus' Great Commission: "Therefore go and make disciples of all [children], baptizing them in the name of the Father and of the Son and of the Holy Spirit, and teaching them to obey everything I have commanded you. And surely I am with you always, to the very end of the age" (Matthew 28:19-20).

> Therefore go and make disciples of all children.

The secret to "training up a child in the way he should go" (Proverbs 22:6) is conveying to our children how precious they are to God. As Deanne whispers to her bright-eyed youngsters, "'There's something that no one else but you can do. Right now, it's a mystery. But when you get older, he'll show you what it is, and then it will be an adventure!'"

Homebodies Hint. Take your children in your arms and let them know how precious they are to you and to their heavenly Father.

41

Setting the Right Example

Walking the talk

*F*lashing lights in my rearview mirror brought the wonderful daydream I had been enjoying to a crashing halt. Dismayed, I slowed the minivan and, signaling, carefully pulled off onto the interstate shoulder.

"What's the matter, Mommy?" My two young daughters perked up, ever sensitive to the frustrated sigh or muttered breath.

Hundreds of thoughts batted around my brain—not the least of which was "I can't afford this!"—as I watched the trooper unfold himself from his cruiser, pull out his ticket book and begin scribbling down my license plate number.

Hastily checking to make sure both girls had their seatbelts fastened—and thus avoiding another $100 fine—I struggled to keep my infamous temper in check. One of the legal authorities I have been teaching my children to respect now stood at my window.

You would have been proud of me. Although I come from a long line of verbally aggressive people, I was attentive. I was cordial. I didn't argue (unless you count the silent screaming inside my head).

What followed was a series of shocks. First, the trooper told me how fast I was going. ("There's no way—his radar must add another twenty miles per hour! Either that, or my speedometer is off. I bet that's it. This minivan was ancient when we bought it. I knew that salesman was crooked.")

Then he cited me. ("You must be kidding! I haven't had a ticket in almost ten years—what happened to warnings? Look at me; a practically innocent mom with two little girls. Why isn't this cop out catching some real criminals? There's no justice in this world.")

Finally, he showed me how much my lead-footed preoccupation would cost. ("I can't believe this! When did fines go up? Do you know how many groceries I could buy with this money? Aarggh!")

Fortunately no one actually knew I was flipping out. All that my extremely attentive little girls heard was me being *very* polite to Mr. Policeman. After all, Grandpa—the very one we were driving to visit—is an officer too. (Mentioning that didn't get me out of the ticket, however.)

Pulling back onto the highway, I was bombarded with questions from the backseat.

"Are we going home?"

"Are you mad?"

"Are you going to tell Daddy?" Oh, man—I forgot about my husband. ("Aarggh!")

Will we practice what we preach?

Outwardly I was calm as I concentrated on the freeway ahead. I was also quiet.

> My children got to see firsthand that I'm not perfect.

Karen and Carrie got the message that we'd talk later. And after a few law-abiding miles we did.

It was an expensive lesson, but my children got to see firsthand that I'm not perfect. Once I got my fiery emotions under control, the teachable moment opened up. "I messed up, girls. I got in trouble because I was driving too fast, and now I have to pay a fine. It hurts, but it has to be done. There are always consequences to our actions, whether good or bad."

My daughters listened, nodded and absorbed. Watching such a scene play out before them planted the message deeper than any abstract illustration ever could have.

When we find ourselves called on the carpet by one of the very figures we grill our children to respect, it is the kids who are watching closest. Will we practice what we preach? Or will we pose and preen ourselves, avoiding responsibility when it is thrust in our faces?

Well beneath the speed limit, I plotted the minivan onward to Grandpa's house. A small voice piped up from the back. "Don't pull over to the side of the road anymore, Mommy," my preschooler counseled. "I don't want you to be sad again."

Sad. Yes, I'd rather her see me sad than breathing fire.

"That's okay, honey. I'm driving the right way now, paying attention and keeping safe." Quiet descended.

The peace lasted approximately 2.6 miles longer.

"I have to go potty!"

And we kept moving on down the highway—on cruise control.

Homebodies Hint. Tell your children about a time you took responsibility when you messed up and what you learned from that experience.

42

Feeding
Your Spirit

Maintaining your
personal devotional time

*B*efore she had kids, Debi enjoyed a kind of daily communion with God that most of us only dream about. "I used to have the most wonderful devotional times, spending several hours playing hymns on my flute, cross-referencing verses, absorbing what the Lord had to say to me," she remembers.

"About halfway through my first pregnancy, my husband Neal read the book of 1 John to the baby every night, because he not only wanted her to know his voice, he wanted her to get a good start with Scripture.

"Of course, once Elizabeth was on the other side of the womb, everything fell apart," Debi admits. "It took all our effort just to keep up with laundry, so these great plans for the spiritual nourishment of our child fell by the wayside. I used to be involved with Bible studies, go to retreats, enjoy conferences. But once the baby was born, I couldn't afford it or didn't have the energy. Plus, I was such a perfectionist, I figured if I couldn't have my two- or three-hour block of devotional time, why bother? So I became spiritually emaciated. It took awhile for me to understand how to adapt my spiritual life to include motherhood.

"Now instead of feasting on a banquet of uninterrupted hours of devotional time, I grab his nourishing energy bars throughout the day." Debi takes opportunities to focus on her Lord where she finds them: listening to Christian radio while she washes dishes, surfing online Bible studies, "dancing like David" with Elizabeth and her son, Andrew.

> It took awhile to adapt my spiritual life to motherhood.

She also tries getting up earlier, to squeeze in some prayer and Bible study before Elizabeth and Andrew wake up. Sometimes it works; sometimes it doesn't. "I frequently became irritated when the kids would interrupt me, regardless of my starting earlier and earlier. Then I realized two things: (1) There's nothing sacred about the morning. I could have my devotionals any time, or in segments throughout the day. (2) I don't have to stop just because the kids found me. They need to see me reading my own Bible, not just their children's picture Bible; to know that I'm an individual, with my own relationship with the Lord."

To maintain sanity and direction, every at-home parent needs to connect with their Father on a daily basis. After Shauna's husband goes to work each morning, she gets her young sons settled, eating breakfast and watching a PBS show as they ease into the day. "I go to my room, kneel by the bed and spend time in prayer. Once in a great while, the kids will come in if they need something. But that's okay. I want them to see me on my knees praying. I just chuckle to God, 'Excuse me,' go get what they need, then tell my kids that I need to talk to God some more, so I'll be out in a minute.

"All of my life, I have had an intellectual relationship with God, compartmentalizing him wherever it was convenient," Shauna admits. "I did not even know what it meant to have a 'personal' relationship with Jesus, even though many of my Christian counterparts talked in great detail of their relationship and how it affected their life. They might as well have spoken Greek, for all I knew!

Kids need to see our personal relationship with God.

"I spent many years doubting considerably that Jesus could be the *only* way, and the church I was raised in only compounded my doubts. I read lots of books that would be classified as New Age. I would find an answer that filled me momentarily, but then I was off again on my search, looking for something else.

"It was only when I came to know Jesus and surrendered my whole being—my life, my desires, my everything—and made the conscious decision to have him be Lord of everything about me that the whole world finally fell into place. Now that Jesus is the center of my life (he guides every step I take, every decision I make), my life makes sense. I have an overwhelming peace that I have never experienced before. I am one who was raised in a church, but never knew Christ personally until nearly age thirty.

"He nurtures and matures me, little by little. Every day is an exciting walk with the Lord. I can honestly say that I feel his presence with me at all times.

"One thing I know for sure," Shauna concludes. "Our Father is yearning to know every person on this planet, to have a personal relationship with them through his Son, Jesus Christ. He doesn't collect Christians to fill his ego. He wants us so that we can become the creation he always intended us to be! He yearns to heal us, comfort us, sustain us and give us freedom from the chains this world binds us with."

Homebodies Hint. Whether in the form of banquets or energy bars, daily time with God is essential as we care for the families he gave us. Do you need a spiritual snack right now?

Appendix:
The Stay-at-Home Network

According to recent government statistics, nearly 75 percent of married mothers with children under eighteen work. That means working women who become stay-at-home moms have to take action to avoid feeling isolated.

"The biggest problem I had in my first year as a stay-at-home mom was the loneliness," Charlotte says. "I had no connection to any other stay-at-home moms because I had been in the work-for-pay force for two decades. It was a rough year, but I slowly found my network and have been firmly attached ever since."

Found my network. That's the key phrase in Charlotte's letter. She discovered ways to link up with other like-minded moms.

A smart prospective at-home parent will start her search for support long before she leaves the workplace. As in so many other areas in life, having a plan will work to your benefit. Tell yourself, "This is how I'm going to carve out time to spend with friends" or "I'm going to check out local moms' groups in the evenings and on weekends and start building some relationships."

Take action to avoid becoming isolated.

"You will need live adult interaction during the day to keep sane," J.J. advises. "Try to find out if there is a moms' group in your area. Check flyers at church, at the doctor's office and so on, for such groups. Or start your own! It took one lonely mom to start the moms' group I'm with now, and five years later there are close to seventy members.

"Check your newspaper and community centers for classes you can enjoy with your child. I've taken a 'Mommy and Me' swim class at a local community center that was a lot of fun, and I met several moms there. Hospitals also offer great classes, like infant massage.

Start your search for support before you leave the office.

"If you can afford to, join a gym with child-care," J.J. continues. "I recently did this, and it has helped me a great deal. It is something I do for myself, and I get to be around other adults for a couple of hours. My son also enjoys getting out of the house."

If you're only using your computer to help your kids with their school work, you're missing out on one of the greatest support systems available to stay-at-home moms—a worldwide network of like-minded parents. For instance, thousands of women visit my Homebodies website each week, and many of them are headed for the message boards. Within a moderated forum, parents exchange frustrations and successes, encouraging and empowering each other with been-there, done-that advice.

So what *is* a message board? I compare it to a regular bulletin board you pass in a hallway. On the physical bulletin board, someone can pin up a piece of paper, telling what they need. The next person coming down the hall can read what the first wrote, then keep on going. Or they can write their own message on that piece of paper for everyone, including the original writer, to see.

Everyone walking down that hall benefits from reading the advice shared and has the opportunity to share their own thoughts too. That is what a message board is like, except you type your message on a special web page and post it on a virtual board.

The great thing about the Internet is that it really is a worldwide web. On any given day, Homebodies may have visitors from the United States, Canada, Australia, Japan, France or Zimbabwe. The next day we may hear from Sweden, South Africa and Sri Lanka. It's eye-opening to see that no matter where we live, parents share similar concerns and hopes for their children.

Remember that there are hundreds of sites to choose from on the Internet, and you should link up with ones you feel most comfortable with. (I've listed the names and web addresses of several I recommend at the end of this chapter.) But the various comments below will give you an idea of what's going on at Homebodies, where I have done my best to provide a safe atmosphere for you.

"I wanted to say thanks to everyone! I was just rereading the replies you all sent to me awhile back (re: life w/a toddler). I wanted to let you know how much I appreciated your input and support. It's nice to know I'm in such good company as a SAHM! This board is one place I know I can come to and feel validated as a full time mom, in a society that doesn't always recognize the hard work we do each and every day. You all are *great!*"

"I am still adjusting to my new lifestyle, but I can say that I truly feel that this is the right decision. I plan on reading these boards daily, and I would love a few ideas from experienced SAHMs."

"I am one of the working moms trying to get home on this board. I have gotten wonderful advice, tons of laughter, tears, kindness (and some much needed reality checks) on this board from SAHMs, WAHMs [Work-at-Home Moms] and other working moms. I truly feel part of this loving family. You will see that we all have different personalities and views, but we share a common bond—we love our families and want what's right for them in the eyes of the Lord."

"Gracias. Thank you. Merci. Danke. I just wanted to thank you all for all your support and love and guidance over the past months. As you know, I do this periodically so that you all remember how special you are and that you also remember that SAHM's ROCK! I just want you to know that I appreciate that you put up with all my wackiness and opinionatedness (I think I just made that word up but it sounds about right). I want you to close your eyes (not right now—keep reading) spread your arms out really wide and wrap them around yourself and squeeze—that's a hug from me."

Recommended Resources

Let me introduce you to some online organizations you may find helpful. Several also provide print materials, conferences or local support groups.

Homebodies
(www.homebodies.org)
Founder: Cheryl Gochnauer
Address: P.O. Box 6883, Lee's Summit, MO 64064-6883
Phone: (816) 524-4716

Caring at Home
(www.momsnetwork.com/suites/
parentchild/caringathome)
Founders: Brigitte Thompson and
Stacey Hammett
Phone: (802) 288-8040
Fax: (802) 288-8041

Cheapskate Monthly
(www.cheapskatemonthly.com)
Founder: Mary Hunt
Address: P.O. Box 2135, Paramount, CA 90723-8135
Phone: (562) 630-6474
Fax: (562) 630-3433

Crown Financial Ministries
(www.crown.org)
Founder: Larry Burkett
Address: P.O. Box 100, Gainesville, GA 30503-0100
Phone: (770) 534-1000

Dr. Laura.Com
(www.drlaura.com)
Founder: Dr. Laura Schlessinger
Address: P.O. Box 8120, Van Nuys, CA 91409
Phone: (800) 375-2872
Fax: (818) 461-5140

The Dollar Stretcher
(www.stretcher.com)
Founder: Gary Foreman
Address: PO Box 14160, Bradenton, FL 34280-4160
Phone: (941) 794-1183
Fax: (941) 794-1682

The Family Corner
(www.familycorner.com)
Founder: Amanda Formaro
Address: 8032 22nd Avenue, #122, Kenosha, WI 53181
Phone: (262) 877-8809

Hearts at Home
(www.hearts-at-home.org)
Founder: Jill Savage
Address: 900 W. College Avenue, Normal, IL 61761
Phone: (309) 888-MOMS
Fax: (309) 888-4525

MainStreetMom.com
(www.mainstreetmom.com)
Founders: Mia Cronan and
Crystal Dupry
Address: 5 Northwood Road,
Greensburg, PA 15601
Phone: (724) 838-0747
Fax: (724) 838-0748

Maxed Out!
(www.maxedout.net)
Founder: Debi Stack
Address: P.O. Box 11805, Kansas
City, MO 64138
Fax: (816) 524-8678

Miserly Moms
(www.miserlymoms.com)
Founder: Jonni McCoy
Address: P.O. Box 49182, Colorado
Springs, CO 80949

Moms in Touch International
(www.momsintouch.org)
Founder: Fern Nichols
Address: P.O. Box 1120, Poway, CA
92074-1120
Phone: (800) 949-MOMS

Moms Network
(www.momsnetwork.com)
Founder: Cyndi Webb
Address: P.O. Box 238, Rosemount,
MN 55068
Phone: (651) 423-4036
Fax: (651) 322-1702

Mothers & More
(www.mothersandmore.org)
Founder: Joanne Brundage
Address: P.O. Box 31, Elmhurst, IL
60126
Phone: (800) 223-9399

Mothers at Home
(www.mah.org)
Founders: Janet Dittmer, Cheri
Loveless and Linda Burton
Address: 9493-C Silver King Ct.,
Fairfax, VA 22031
Phone: (800) 783-4666

Mothers of Preschoolers
(www.mops.org)
Founder: Elisa Morgan
Address: P.O. Box 10220, Denver,
CO 80250-2200
Phone: (800) 929-1287 or (303) 733-5353

National Association of At-Home Mothers
(www.athomemothers.com)
Founder: Jeanette Lisefski
Address: 406 E. Buchanan Ave.,
Fairfield, IA 52556
Fax: (641) 469-3068

National Center for Fathering
(www.fathers.com)
Founder: Ken Canfield
Address: P.O. Box 413888, Kansas
City, MO 64141
Phone: (800) 593-DADS
Fax: (913) 384-4665

National Home Education Network
(www.nhen.org)
Address: P.O. Box 41067, Long
Beach, CA 90853
Fax: (413) 581-1463

Parents and Teens
(www.parentsandteens.com)
Founder: Patricia Chadwick
Address: 22 Williams St., Batavia,
NY 14020
Phone/Fax: (716) 343-2810

Proverbs 31 Ministry
(www.proverbs31.org)
Founder: Sharon Jaynes
Address: P.O. Box 17155, Charlotte,
NC 28227
Phone: (877) P31-HOME.

Work-at-Home Moms
(www.wahm.com)
Founder: Cheryl Demas
Address: Box 366, Folsom, CA 95763
Phone: (916) 985-2078

About the Author

I hope you have enjoyed the conversational tone of Stay-at-Home Handbook. If you would like to continue this discussion at your upcoming parenting or marriage-based retreat, conference or seminar, contact me for details regarding my speaking ministry at:

Homebodies.Org, LLC
Attn: Event Coordinator
P.O. Box 6883
Lee's Summit, MO 64064-6883
Phone: (816) 524-4716
E-mail: cheryl@homebodies.org

For a listing of suggested presentation topics, visit my website: <www.homebodies.org/contact.htm>.